Edinburgh
and the Borders

AA Publishing

Produced by AA Publishing

© The Automobile Association 1997
Maps © The Automobile Association 1997

First published 1997

Published by AA Publishing (a trading name of Automobile Association Developments Limited, whose registered office is Norfolk House, Priestley Road, Basingstoke, Hampshire RG24 9NY; registered number 1878835).

ISBN 0 7495 1492 2

A CIP catalogue record for this book is available from the British Library.

Designer: Stuart Perry

Colour separation by BTB, Digital Imaging, Whitchurch, Hampshire

Printed and bound by George Over Ltd, Rugby

EDINBURGH AND THE BORDERS

Edinburgh inevitably dominates the counties of West Lothian, Midlothian and East Lothian. The name Lothian itself originally belonged to an ancient kingdom which was often under the sway of the English kings of Northumbria, until King Malcolm II of Scots defeated the Northumbrians in a decisive battle in the 11th century. Edinburgh eventually became the capital of Scotland and today, below its impregnable castle rock, is one of Britain's most attractive, civilised and enjoyable cities, dominated by its ancient castle and the home of the country's most prestigious arts festival.

Covering the former counties of Berwick, Roxburgh, Selkirk and Peebles, with a bit of Midlothian thrown in, the Scottish Borders were for centuries the war-torn land north of the border with England, fought over from Roman times to the 17th century, trodden and devastated by armies, and restless with raiding and rustling even in times of peace or truce. Hermitage Castle's grim and solitary hold and the ruined abbeys of Melrose, Jedburgh, Kelso and Dryburgh bear gaunt witness to a violent past in what is today pleasant farming, forest and hill country, known for peaceable tweeds and knitted goods. Towns like Kelso, Hawick and Selkirk keep up their historic 'common riding' customs and Peebles and Galashiels are textile centres. The Tweed and the Teviot are famous fishing rivers. Sir Walter Scott's home at Abbotsford can be visited below the magical Eildon Hills. To the west are the remains of the great Forest of Ettrick and John Buchan's favourite Tweedsmuir Hills, while Traquair, near Innerleithen, is one of the most romantic houses in all Britain. To the north lies the lonely moorland of the Lammermuirs.

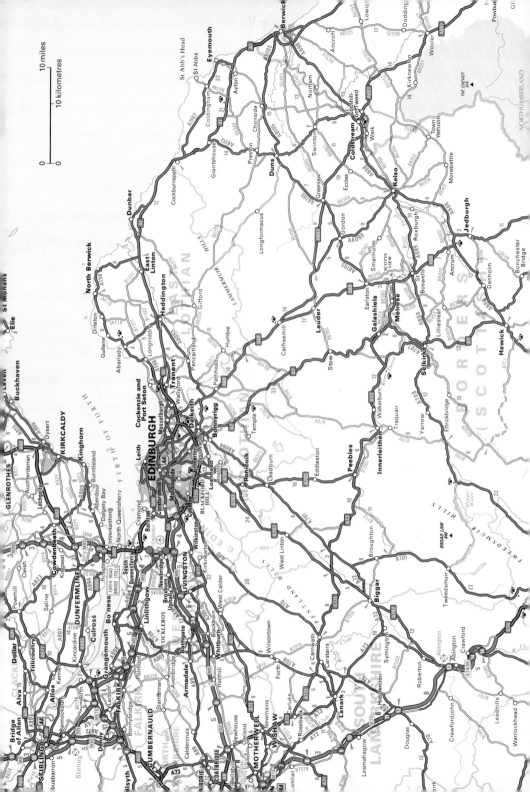

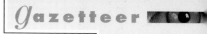

gazetteer

This tiny and remote village in the Lammermuir Hills is situated on the Whiteadder Water. In the parish church is preserved the tomb of a prioress, portraying her pet dog, from the former 12th-century abbey church. Edinshall Broch, a prehistoric stone tower near by, is a rare example outside the Northern Highlands.

Once the trading port for Haddington until the river silted up, this long and scattered village has a medieval church with fine stained-glass windows. Near by are good sandy beaches and dunes: Aberlady Bay Nature Reserve lies east, with good bird-watching on the saltmarshes. Nearby Gosford House (limited opening) is an impressive Robert Adam mansion.

This is a charming and wide-ranging collection, with cars and motorcycles from 1896, cycles from 1863 and commercial vehicles, historic British military vehicles, advertising signs and automobilia.
   Open all year, daily. Closed 25 Dec & 1 Jan.

Ancrum stands round a green on the River Ale near a junction with the River Teviot. There are Iron Age and Roman hillforts in the neighbourhood, and on the banks of the Ale are a number of caves, used perhaps in ancient Border warfare. Away to the north of the village is Ancrum Moor, or Lilliard's Edge, the scene of one of the last conflicts, fought in 1545, and a Roman road leading through the site.

Now a dormitory suburb of Edinburgh, Balerno was once known for its corn and papermills, powered by Water of Leith. Malleny House incorporates an old royal hunting lodge and a garden.

The delightful gardens are set around a 17th-century house. There is a good selection of shrub roses, a woodland garden, and a group of four clipped yews, the survivors of a group of 12 which were planted in 1603. The National Bonsai Collection for Scotland is also here.
   Open all year, daily. House not open.

A basalt outcrop, 350ft (106m) high, in the Firth of Forth, Bass Rock acts as a landmark visible for miles. There is a lighthouse, and the rock provides nesting for huge colonies of seabirds.

The Treaty of Birgham (1290) established details of Scotland's independence. 'Go to Birgham!' was a local pejorative exclamation, Birgham being the furthest south possible without crossing the border.

ABBEY ST BATHANS
VILLAGE OFF B6355, 5 MILES (8KM) N OF DUNS

ABERLADY
VILLAGE ON A198, 6 MILES (9.5KM) SW OF NORTH BERWICK

Myreton Motor Museum
TEL: 01875 870288

ANCRUM
VILLAGE ON B6400, 3 MILES (5KM) NW OF JEDBURGH

BALERNO
VILLAGE OFF A70, 4 MILES (6.5KM) SE OF EDINBURGH

Malleny Garden
TEL: 0131 449 2283

BASS ROCK
ISLAND IN FIRTH OF FORTH

BIRGHAM
VILLAGE ON A698, 3 MILES (5KM) W OF COLDSTREAM

*B*eecraigs Country Park offers a wide range of activities, including a climbing wall and target archery course. The walk takes in a wonderful viewpoint, a trout farm and a deer farm.

Grid ref: NT006746

INFORMATION

The walk is about 3½ miles (5.5km) long.
Tracks and paths mostly have good surfaces, with one short stretch of open grassy hill.
Two sets of steps at the deer farm.
Dogs should be kept on leads.

A range of information is available at the Park Centre.
Refreshments available at the Centre.
Cafés in Linlithgow.
Picnic tables at Balvormie near an attractive pond.
Toilets at the Park Centre, at Balvormie and in Linlithgow.

START

Beecraigs Park Centre is 2 miles (3km) south of Linlithgow. Take a minor road from the west end of Linlithgow, signed 'Beecraigs Country Park', then follow signs for Beecraigs Loch, turning left then right to reach the Park Centre.

DIRECTIONS

From the Centre, return past the entrance, cross the road and take the track opposite, signed 'Balvormie Walk'. In 100yds (91.5m) take the left fork past a gate on to a forest track. Follow the track for nearly ½ mile (1km) to reach the 'trim track'. Just beyond this is the Balvormie car park. Cross the road, signed 'Cockleroy Walk' and take the path immediately in front of the toilet block to re-enter the woods.

About 250yds (229m) after the toilets, where a blue waymark points back the way you have come, turn right onto a narrower path down across a small stream and continue to a junction. Turn left to reach a road, cross over (the Cockleroy car park is on the right) and continue on the path opposite (another blue waymark). At the edge of the wood, cross a stile and walk up to the summit of Cockleroy (cairn and a viewpoint indicator). When you have enjoyed the view, return to the stile and retrace your steps to the Cockleroy car park, across the road, and back to Balvormie. Cross the car park and from its

WHAT TO LOOK OUT FOR

The Cockleroy view stretches from coast to coast. In the woods you may see roe deer, rabbits, brown hares and perhaps a fox, and birds include great spotted woodpeckers.

right side cross the stream and turn left along a wide track fringed by broad-leaved trees. Keep on this track for about ½ mile (1km), to reach the next road. Turn left for 50yds (45m) and turn right on the road to the trout farm. Pass the anglers' lodge and reach the trout farm, leaving it by crossing the bridge and climbing the steps to the top of the dam. Turn right along the dam and then left in the woods, keeping the loch on your left. Part way along the loch at a junction, turn right, signed 'Deer Farm'.

On the summit of Cockleroy

Climb and descend steps to enter the walkway through the deer farm, continuing round to the left, then climb and descend more steps to return to the Park Centre.

Cockleroy

Cockleroy, which has the remains of an ancient fort, is only 912ft (278m) high, but commands an exceptional view. On very clear days you can see as far as Goat Fell on Arran, the Bass Rock to the east, Edinburgh, and across the Firth of Forth. The viewpoint indicator will help you identify all the places. Take a pair of binoculars for added enjoyment.

The Trout Farm

The fish bred here are used for stocking rivers and lochs in the area, providing sport for anglers, and trout can also be bought for the table.

The Deer Farm

Red deer, our largest native mammals, are bred here for their meat, which can be bought at the Park Centre. The stags have been 'de-antlered' to save them injuring themselves or the hinds.

Young are born in June, and in October during the 'rut' the stags can be heard roaring as they prepare to mate.

BROUGHTON
VILLAGE ON A701, 4 MILES (6KM) E OF PEEBLES

Broughton Place
TEL: 01899 830234

A house in Broughton village

This Tweed Valley village was where the writer John Buchan, Lord Tweedsmuir, spent many holidays. Bigger Water and the Broughton Burn unite to flow together into the Tweed to the south-east of the village. Beside the ruined old church, in the cemetery, is a restored vault, thought to be the remains of a cell, founded in the 7th century by St Llolan, a Pictish saint.

The house was designed by Sir Basil Spence in 1938, in the style of a 17th-century Scottish tower house. The drawing room and main hall are open to the public, and have paintings and crafts by living British artists for sale. The gardens are open and give fine views of the Tweeddale Hills. A full programme of exhibitions is available on request.

Open: gallery end Mar–mid-Oct & mid-Nov–late Dec, most days.

This charming fishing village is tucked under steep sandstone cliffs, sheltered by Ross Point, to the south. Two treaties between Scotland and England, in 1384, and again in 1497, were signed here.

Carter Bar is the border point between England and Scotland on the A68. Located on the crest of the Cheviot ridge, this was part of the lawless Middle March region. The view from here is famous, and extends towards the Cheviot itself and well into the Lowlands, with the triple-peaked Eildon Hills appearing in the distance. The last Border battle, the Redeswire Raid, took place here in 1575. To the east are the notable camp and earthworks of Chew Green, situated just inside Northumberland, across the English border. Here is the earliest of the Roman roads into Scotland, the Dere Street, built by Agricola.

There is a local connection with Sir Walter Scott and a memorial window at nearby Caddenfoots church. Vineyards laid out by the Duke of Buccleuch's head gardener here in the 1860s were heated by 5 miles (8km) of cast-iron pipes.

This mainly 18th-century village lies inland from the sandy Coldingham Bay. A priory founded in the 7th century was repeatedly destroyed and was finally partially blown up by Cromwell in 1648. The remains form part of a church, some 13th-century work having been preserved. The 19th-century discovery of a female skeleton embedded upright in the south transept was written about by Sir Walter Scott. The ruined Fast Castle up the coast featured in Scott's *Bride of Lammermuir*.

A town on the busy A697 with a ford, used for numerous English invasions until the present bridge was built in 1776. A tablet, placed on the bridge in 1926, records the fact that in 1787 Robert Burns first visited England by this route. Up to 1856 marriages were frequently performed at the former toll-house at the Scottish end of the bridge.

The town is associated with the Coldstream Guards; the name originally was the nickname for the Second Foot Guards. There are rideouts in August to commemorate Flodden. The Hirsel (1640s) is the family seat of the Earls of Home, pronounced 'Hume'.

The Hirsel is the seat of the Home family, and its grounds are open all year. The focal point is the Homestead Museum, craft centre and workshops. From there, nature trails lead around the lake, along the Leet Valley and into a wood which is noted for its rhododendrons and azaleas. There are a tea room and picnic areas.

Garden & grounds open all year, daylight hours.

BURNMOUTH
VILLAGE ON A1, 2 MILES (3KM) S OF EYEMOUTH

CARTER BAR
SITE ON A68, 10 MILES (16KM) SE OF JEDBURGH

CLOVENFORDS
VILLAGE ON A72, 3 MILES (5KM) W OF GALASHIELS

COLDINGHAM
VILLAGE ON A1107, 3 MILES (5KM) NW OF EYEMOUTH

COLDSTREAM
SMALL TOWN ON A697, 9 MILES (14.5KM) NE OF KELSO

The Hirsel
TEL: 01890 882834 & 882965

CRAMOND
VILLAGE OFF A90, 5 MILES (8KM) W OF EDINBURGH

The minutes of the local Kirk Session at Cramond make surprisingly scurrilous reading. Those dated 5 August 1660 record that: Margrat Corstoune...gave in a bill of slander against Isbell Wallace...quhairin was conteind that the said Isbell Wallace had said that the said Margrat was a witch or that shee had the carriage of a witch, and a runnagate, and blackned bitch. The said Isbell gave in a bill against Margrat Corstoune quhairin was

Cramond today is a charming place of old white-painted stone cottages that layer steeply down to an ancient quay at the mouth of the River Almond. A ferry boat takes passengers across the narrow estuary to Lord Rosebery's Dalmeny estates. A wooded riverside walk leads past a small boat park to a weir and a ruined mill. A picture-postcard image, perhaps, but one that belies its past.

On the orders of Emperor Antoninus Pius, around AD142 the Romans built a harbour and fort here, at the eastern end of the Empire's northernmost frontier line. Part of the fort can be seen near the church, a mainly 17th-century building on a site used for many, many centuries before that. Note its fine carved gravestones.

Near by are Cramond Tower, a medieval defensive tower, and Cramond House, home of successive lairds of Cramond.

Below it, in the 18th and 19th centuries, the waters of the Almond powered no fewer than five mills. Originally used for corn and cloth, by 1752 they were manufacturing iron nails, spades, hoops, cart axles and so on.

There is little remaining of the highest mills, Peggie's Mill and Dowie's Mill. Cockle Mill, the lowest and closest to the quay where iron was imported and finished products exported, is now a private house. There are traces here of various weirs, a tidal dock and former offices. Cockle Mill was the rolling and slitting mill

described by John Rennie in 1782 as having three water wheels. Storage sheds for coal were built into the hillside, and slag was tipped into the river upstream.

The old workers' cottages have been renovated, while the main forge, Fairafar Mill, is the ruin that stands by the weir – silent testimony to noisier, dirtier days.

Crichton Collegiate Church was built in 1449 by William Crichton, Lord Chancellor of Scotland, at the same time as he was adding to the castle. The two buildings stand apart in a rural position at the head of the Tyne Valley.

The castle dates back to the 14th century, but most of what remains today was built over the following 300 years. A notable feature is the 16th-century wing built by the Earl of Bothwell in Italian style, with an arcade below.

Sir Walter Scott's hero Marmion also passed by:

> That Castle rises on the steep of the green
> Vale of Tyne. . .
> Where alders moist and willows weep
> Yon hear her streams repine.

conteind that the said Margrat had cald her a drunken harlot and lowne.

CRICHTON
VILLAGE OFF B6367, 3 MILES (5KM) S OF PATHHEAD

Crichton Castle
TEL: 0131 668 8800

An archetypal Borders landscape as seen from Carter Bar

 gazetteer

DALKEITH
Town on A68, 6 miles (9.5km) SE of Edinburgh

A busy market town, Dalkeith was once a centre for agriculture and the Lothian coalfields. Dalkeith House is an early classical mansion around an earlier castle (not open).

Edinburgh Butterfly & Insect World
Dobbies Garden Centre, Lasswade
Tel: 0131 663 4932

Richly coloured butterflies from all over the world can be seen flying among exotic plants, trees and flowers. The tropical pools are filled with giant waterlilies and colourful fish, and are surrounded by lush vegetation. Also displayed are scorpions, leaf cutting ants, beetles, tarantulas and other remarkable creatures. There is a unique honeybee display and daily insect handling sessions.
  Open Mar–early Jan, daily.

DALMENY
Village off A90, 1 mile (2km) E of South Queensferry

Dalmeny House, seat of the Earls of Rosebery, overlooks the Firth of Forth in landscaped grounds and replaced the earlier Barnbougle Castle in the 1820s. The house is an excellent example of Tudor Gothic Revival: superb collections include Spanish tapestries and French furniture. Dalmeny Kirk in the estate village is one of the best preserved Norman churches in Britain. Of special interest are the richly carved south doorway, and also the chancel and semi-circular vaulted apse. Some of the carvings represent curious mythological wild beasts. The tower is of more recent date.
  (See also page 79.)

DIRLETON
Village on B1435, 2 miles (3km) W of North Berwick

A charming picture-postcard village of pantiled cottages set about two greens with the extensive remains of the 13th-century Dirleton Castle, destroyed by Cromwell, on a rocky mound behind. The well-tended castle grounds have a 17th-century dovecote and bowling green; the church dates from the same century. Open Arms, a famous inn, over-looks both green and castle.

Dirleton Castle
Tel: 0131 668 8800.

This sturdy castle was raised in the 13th century, probably on the remains of an earlier fortress. The principal building was the impressive three-storeyed round keep or 'drum' tower, supported by a complex arrangement of other towers and walls. In the 14th and 15th centuries the castle was considerably enlarged, to include a chapel with a prison beneath, and a pit-prison hewn from the rock below that. Although a ruin, Dirleton still presents an imposing face to the world and crossing the modern wooden footbridge to the great gatehouse, it is easy to appreciate the difficulties faced by any would-be attacker.
  Dorothea, wife of the rebellious Earl of Gowrie, was probably one of the saddest residents of Dirleton Castle. Her husband was executed in 1585 after a plot to seize Stirling Castle was discovered, and all his lands and castles were taken by King James VI, leaving

Dorothea and her 15 children poverty-stricken. The King granted Dirleton Castle to Gowrie's great rival, the Earl of Arran, who kept it until the castle and its lands were restored to Dorothea almost two years later. Then, in 1600, two of her sons were involved in the mysterious 'Gowrie Conspiracy', when it was alleged that they tried to kill the King. Although the maiming of the corpses of Dorothea's sons was very public, details of the entire affair remained secret.

Open all year, daily. Closed Xmas & New Year.

Drumelzier – pronounced 'Drummelier' – is said to be the burial place of Merlin, the wizard of Arthurian legend. The reputed spot is where the Drumelzier Burn comes down from its wooded dell to join the River Tweed. Of the 16th-century castle, only fragments remain, situated near the river about 1mile (1.5km) to the south-west.

Dirleton Castle is built on a rock outcrop, surrounded by the remains of a moat

DRUMELZIER
Village on B712, 8 miles (13km) SW of Peebles

DRYBURGH

VILLAGE ON B6404, 1 MILE (1.5KM) N OF ST BOSWELLS

DUNBAR

TOWN ON A1087, 27 MILES (43.5KM) E OF EDINBURGH

▸ The incredibly romantic sandstone ruins of Dryburgh Abbey stand amidst stately trees and lawns beside the River Tweed. Founded by David I in 1150, it was frequently damaged during the Border Wars, and mouldered from the 1600s. Ruins of the church, monastic buildings and chapter house are still extant. This is the burial place of Sir Walter Scott and Field Marshal Earl Haig, and is visited by many.

▸ Dunbar is on the North Sea coast with an intricate double harbour dating from its fishing heyday and overlooked by castle ruins. In the 18th century Dunbar was Scotland's main herring port. Converted warehouses, granaries and maltings surround the harbour. A wide High Street has a 17th-century six-sided town house, the oldest civic building in constant use in Scotland. The town is the birthplace of John

The beautiful ruins of Dryburgh Abbey are peacefully situated

Muir, conservationist and founder of the North American National Park system; nearby John Muir Country Park commemorates him.

(See also Picnic: John Muir Country Park, page 58.)

This market town with a castle lies in fertile farmland below Duns Law, a hill on which the town was at one time situated, before being destroyed by the English in 1545.

Motor racing trophies won by Jim Clark are on display, including world championship trophies and Grand Prix awards. Clark was killed in 1968 and his parents gave the trophies to the town. Displays include photographs and a video presentation.

Open Etr–Oct, daily.

DUNS
TOWN ON A6105, 13 MILES (21KM) W OF BERWICK

Jim Clark Room
44 NEWTOWN ST
TEL: 01361 883960

Manderston
TEL: 01361 883450

This grandest of grand houses gives a fascinating picture of Edwardian life both above and below stairs. It was built for the millionaire racehorse owner Sir James Miller, whose family had made their fortune trading with Russia. The original Georgian house was rebuilt between 1903 and 1905. The architect was told to spare no expense, and so the house boasts features such as the world's only silver staircase, modelled on that in the Petit Trianon at Versailles, a ballroom painted in Sir James's racing colours, and painted ceilings. The state rooms are magnificent, and the domestic quarters are also quite lavish. Outside buildings include the handsome stable block and marble dairy, built in the style of a Roman cloister, complete with a fountain. There is also a neo-Scots Baronial head gardener's house. The formal gardens include a woodland garden and lakeside walks, and stunning rhododendrons.

Open early May–late Sep, certain days.

EAST LINTON
SMALL TOWN OFF A1, 6 MILES (10KM) W OF DUNBAR

This small town on the River Tyne has a 16th-century bridge which carried the Edinburgh–London mail road. Downstream, the river powers Preston Mill, a restored 18th-century corn mill.

Two miles (3km) outside the town on the river is the ruined Hailes Castle.

(See also Picnic: John Muir Country Park, page 58.)

Hailes Castle
TEL: 0131 668 8800

The castle was a fortified manor house of the Gourlays and Hepburns. Bothwell brought Mary, Queen of Scots here when they were fleeing from Borthwick Castle. The substantial ruins include a 16th-century chapel, the original water gates and a dungeon.

Open at all reasonable times.

Preston Mill
TEL: 01620 860426

This is the oldest working water-driven corn mill to survive in Scotland, and was last used commercially in 1957. It has a conical roof and red pantiles. There is an old mill pond with ducks. A short walk leads to Phantassie Doocot (dovecote), built for 500 birds.

Open May–Sep, daily; wknds in Oct.

EDNAM
VILLAGE ON B6461, 2 MILES (3KM) N OF KELSO

This village was the birthplace, in 1700, of James Thomson, who wrote the words of 'Rule Britannia', and of Henry Lyte, author of 'Abide with Me'.

EILDON HILLS
HILLS S OF MELROSE

These triple-peaked volcanic mounds, named Trimontium by the Romans, (1,385ft/421m), are a 4-mile (6.5-km) walk from Melrose. The Romans established an important communications centre on Eildon Hill North. The hills are the legendary resting place of King Arthur and his knights, sleeping under a spell.

EDINBURGH

This beautiful capital city, known as either 'Auld Reekie' or 'Athens of the north', is the administrative, legal and financial centre of Scotland, with three universities, fine buildings and abundant parks. Edinburgh has a glorious setting, with unexpected views of the sea and hills wherever you happen to be, and a skyline dominated by the great crag on which the castle stands. The city stretches from the port of Leith to Queensferry and the Forth Bridges. It is essentially non-industrial, although there is a brewing and distilling tradition, and the 20th century has seen much urban expansion. With its renowned International Festival and excellent museums it is a cultured and fascinating place, which retains a strong sense of autonomy.

Founded on the defensive Castle Rock and well established by the 13th century, it became Scotland's capital in 1532. Reformation concepts found support in the 1550s with Presbyterianism dominating by the late 1600s. The Union of the Crowns (1603) and the Union of the Parliaments (1707) shifted prestige to London, although Edinburgh retained control of the Church and Scotland's legal and educational systems, ensuring its status as a capital city.

EDINBURGH
CITY ON A1, 413 MILES (661KM) N OF LONDON

The city has two distinct parts: the narrow streets of the unremittingly medieval Old Town and the spacious squares and terraces of the Georgian New Town. The Old Town sprawls down the hill from the ancient fortress of Edinburgh Castle, set high above the city, to the Palace of Holyroodhouse and the adjacent abbey, a stretch lined with tall stone tenement buildings with atmospheric wynds and closes leading off, known as the Royal Mile. Some of Edinburgh's best-known monuments are here, including sombre St Giles Cathedral, Parliament House, now housing the Law Courts, and John Knox's House. There are fine churches and secular buildings, some occupied by museums devoted to Edinburgh and its history. Near by, the open spaces to the Lawnmarket and the Grassmarket recall medieval times, while the neighbouring University of Edinburgh buildings and Scotland's

East Princes Street Gardens awash with crocuses

National Library and Royal Museum represent intellectual life. North of the castle, across gardens formed by draining the old North Loch, lies the splendid New Town, built on a grid pattern between the 1770s and 1830s. Princes Street faces the castle, providing one of Europe's finest city views, although other New Town streets are architecturally better preserved. Along Princes Street lie fine Georgian civic buildings, among them Register House, the Royal Academy and the National Gallery of Scotland, while the Victorian Scott Monument gives a bird's-eye view of the city centre, also obtainable from Calton Hill near by. The New Town's elegant streets spread north down the hill towards the Firth of Forth, with the Royal Botanic Gardens, one of Edinburgh's numerous parks and recreational areas.

Edinburgh, as a major tourist centre, is well provided with hotels, restaurants and other facilities, including some modern business and conference centres and a fine new Opera House. Shopping is more than adequate, with many specialist shops tucked off the beaten track. There is a full range of sports amenities and other entertainment, although clearly Edinburgh shows its best face to the visitor during the Festival.

Brass Rubbing Centre
TRINITY APSE, CHALMERS
CLOSE, HIGH ST
TEL: 0131 556 4364

▶ Housed in the historic, 15th-century remnant of Trinity Apse, the Centre offers the chance to make your own rubbing from a wide range of replica monumental brasses and Pictish stones. Tuition is available. Materials are available for those wanting to experiment; a small charge is made for their use.

Open all year, most days.

Camera Obscura
CASTLEHILL, ROYAL MILE
TEL: 0131 226 3709

▶ Step inside this magical 1850s 'cinema' for a unique experience of Edinburgh. As the lights go down a brilliant moving image of the surrounding city appears. The scene changes as a guide operates the camera's system of revolving lenses and mirrors. As the panorama unfolds the guide tells the story of the city's historic past. Also of interest is the Rooftop Terrace, and exhibitions on International Holography, Pinhole Photography and Victorian Edinburgh.

Open all year, daily. Closed 25 Dec.

City Art Centre
2 MARKET ST
TEL: 0131 529 3993

▶ The City Art Centre houses the city's permanent fine art collection, and stages a constantly changing programme of temporary exhibitions drawn from all parts of the world. It has six floors of display galleries (linked by an escalator), a shop, café and facilities for disabled visitors.

Open all year, most days.

Buildings from four different periods make up the splendid ruins at Craigmillar, situated 2 miles (3km) south-east of Edinburgh. A simple L-plan tower house was built here in the late 14th century, of red-grey sandstone. In the 1420s, this sturdy tower was fortified by the addition of a 28-foot (8.5-m) wall with round towers at the corners, which ran all the way around it. Another set of walls and other buildings were added in the 16th and 17th centuries, including a chapel and kitchens, the remains of which can still be seen.

Although Craigmillar is a good example of a late medieval fortress, it is perhaps better known for its role in history. The first significant bloody act at Craigmillar was the murder of the Earl of Mar by a jealous brother in 1477. It was attacked and seriously damaged by the Earl of Hereford for Henry VIII in 1544, but was sufficiently repaired for Mary, Queen of Scots to retreat there following the murder of a favourite secretary in 1566. While Mary grieved for her loss, her noblemen plotted revenge. It is not known whether Mary was a party to the plot, but a pact was signed that resulted in the murder of Mary's estranged husband, Lord Darnley. While convalescing from a disease, his house was blown up. When his body was recovered, it was found that Darnley had been strangled before the explosion.

Open all year, daily. Closed certain days in winter, 25–26 Dec & 1–3 Jan.

Craigmillar Castle
TEL: 0131 668 8800

Craigmillar Castle is linked to a notorious incident in the life of Mary, Queen of Scots

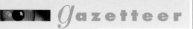

Edinburgh Castle
TEL: 0131 668 8800

Edinburgh Castle dominates the city skyline

There was no capital city of Scotland, as such, until the end of the Middle Ages. Before that, Scotland's capital was wherever the king and his court happened to be. But the magnificent fortress squatting firmly on its plug of rock was a great favourite with Scottish kings, and has played a vital role in history on many occasions. It changed hands several times when the Scots were fighting for independence from England under Robert the Bruce, and became a royal residence under the Stuart kings.

Today, it is a museum – it houses the Scottish National War

Memorial and the Scottish crown jewels – and is the venue for the spectacular annual Edinburgh Military Tattoo. It still dominates the ancient city from its rocky pinnacle, and even though it has been battered and bruised through the centuries, it remains one of the most impressive and best-known castles in the world.

The origins of Edinburgh Castle are shrouded in mystery. Although the great rock on which the castle stands would probably have attracted earlier strongholds, there is no archaeological evidence to prove the site was used earlier than the 11th century. Malcolm III, before his death in 1093, raised a wooden fortress here and his son, David I, built a church to the memory of his mother in the 1120s. The tiny chapel is the oldest surviving building in the castle. Thereafter, Edinburgh became an important gamepiece in the struggles between Edward I and Robert the Bruce in the late 13th century. Edward seized it in 1296, bombarding it with huge boulders from his great war machines. The garrison surrendered after only eight days, and Edward installed 350 of his own soldiers to hold it securely.

The Argyle Battery at Edinburgh Castle

In 1313 the Earl of Moray, acting for Bruce, scaled the daunting cliffs with only 30 men and routed the English. Bruce then ordered that the castle be utterly destroyed, so that it could never again be used by Edward's forces. He underestimated Edward's tenacity, for a few years later Edward retook the site, and set about repairing the damage, even planting gardens and orchards in anticipation of a lengthy stay. But the Scots were undeterred, and in 1341 a small party of Scottish soldiers disguised themselves as merchants and quickly ambushed the startled garrison.

The vast sprawl of the castle contains buildings from many centuries. The fine half-moon battery and portcullis gate date from the 1570s, while the splendid Great Hall and the handsome palace were built for James IV in the early 16th century.

An 'Honours of the Kingdom' exhibition tells the story and history of the Scottish crown jewels. There is still a military presence in the castle, and some areas cannot be visited.

Open all year, daily.

Edinburgh Zoo
CORSTORPHINE RD
(2M W ON A8)
TEL: 0131 334 9171

Set in 80 acres of hillside parkland, Edinburgh Zoo houses Scotland's largest animal collection with over 1,000 animals including many endangered species. The zoo has the world's largest penguin enclosure; four different species and almost 180 penguins altogether can be seen here. There are daily 'penguin parades' from April to September, and October if weather permits. Other attractions include animal handling classes, brass-rubbing and a new Darwin Maze, named after naturalist Charles Darwin and based on the theme of evolution. Panoramic views of Edinburgh and the surrounding countryside can also be enjoyed here. The zoo is an ideal family venue, especially as there is a family ticket available.

Open all year, daily.

General Register House
(EAST END OF PRINCES ST)
TEL: 0131 535 1314

The headquarters of the Scottish Record Office and respository for the national archives of Scotland, designed by Robert Adam and founded in 1774. The historical and legal search rooms are available to researchers, and changing exhibitions are held. No charge is made for historical searches.

Open all year, most days. Closed certain BHs & part of Nov.

Georgian House
7 CHARLOTTE SQ
TEL: 0131 225 2160

The house is part of Robert Adam's splendid north side of Charlotte Square, the epitome of Edinburgh New Town architecture. The lower floors of No 7 have been handsomely restored in the style of around 1800, when the house was built. It gives a vivid impression of Georgian life, in both the grand public rooms and the servants' areas. Visitors can watch videos on life in the Georgian house, and in the New Town.

Open Apr–Oct, daily.

Gladstone's Land
477B LAWNMARKET
TEL: 0131 226 5856

Built in 1620, this six-storey tenement, once the house of a prosperous Edinburgh merchant, still has its arcaded front – a rare feature now. Visitors can also see unusual tempera paintings on the walls and ceilings. It is furnished as a typical home of a 17th-century merchant, complete with ground-floor shop front and goods of the period.

Open Apr–Oct, daily.

Huntly House
142 CANONGATE
TEL: 0131 529 4143

This is one of the best-preserved 16th-century buildings in the Old Town. It was built in 1570 and later became the headquarters of the Incorporation of Hammermen. It is now the main museum of local history, and has collections of silver, glassware, pottery, other items such as street signs, along with a collection relating to Field Marshal Earl Haig, a World War I general.

Open all year, most days.

The house is traditionally associated with John Knox the Reformer and contains an exhibition about his life and times. He is said to have died in the house, which was built by the goldsmith to Mary, Queen of Scots. Renovation work has revealed the original floor in the Oak Room, and a magnificent painted ceiling.

Open all year, most days. Closed Xmas.

John Knox House
THE NETHERBOW,
43–45 HIGH ST
TEL: 0131 556 9579

The museum illustrates the history and everyday life of Scotland. A gallery displays 'Dynasty: the Royal House of Stewart' – 300 years of Stewart rule in Scotland, illustrated by portraits and objects from the Scottish national collections.

Open all year, daily. Closed 25–26 Dec & 1–2 Jan.

Museum of Antiquities
1 QUEEN ST
TEL: 0131 225 7534

One of the first museums of its kind, it was reopened in 1986 after major expansion and reorganisation. It has a wonderful collection of toys, games and other belongings of children through the ages, to delight visitors both old and young.

Open all year, most days.

Museum of Childhood
42 HIGH ST (ROYAL MILE)
TEL: 0131 529 4142

Recognised as one of Europe's best smaller galleries, the National Gallery of Scotland occupies a handsome neo-classical building designed by William Playfair. It contains a notable collection of works by Old Masters, Impressionists and Scottish artists. Among them are the 'Bridgewater Madonna' by Raphael, Constable's 'Dedham Vale', and works by Titian, Velazquez, Van Gogh and Gauguin. Drawings, watercolours and original prints by Turner, Goya, Blake and others are shown on request, at certain times.

Open all year, daily. Closed 25–26 Dec & 1–2 Jan.

National Gallery of Scotland
THE MOUND
TEL: 0131 556 8921

Designed in 1807 and erected on Calton Hill, the monument dominates the east end of Princes Street. Visitors climbing to the top will enjoy superb views of the city. Every day except Sunday the time ball drops at 1pm as the gun at the castle goes off.

Open all year, most days.

Nelson Monument
CALTON HILL
TEL: 0131 556 2716

The museum tells the story of the village and its people. It looks at fishing, other sea trades, customs and superstitions. There are displays on the development of this tightly-knit community, its leisure activities and choirs. The story is told through reconstructed sets of fisherfolk, objects, photographs, first-hand written and spoken accounts of people's lives. The museum also features 'hands-on' exhibits, music and video.

Open all year, daily.

Newhaven Heritage Museum
24 PIER PLACE, NEWHAVEN
TEL: 0131 551 4165

Lauriston Castle

CRAMOND RD SOUTH,
DAVIDSON'S MAINS
(NW OUTSKIRTS OF
EDINBURGH, JUST E OF
CRAMOND)
TEL: 0131 336 2060

A concealed stairway leads
from one corner of the Oak
Room to a small chamber in
the tower wall. It may have
been used as a hideaway,
but a spy-hole, blocked
when a new ceiling was
added in 1827, suggests a
more sinister purpose.

A particular nightmare of school days for some of us can be directly attributed to Lauriston Castle, for it was John Napier, the son of its first owner, who invented logarithms! The house, set in 30 acres (12ha) of lovely parkland and peaceful gardens, has considerably more charm for most people than the mathematics, however.

A number of notable Scots have called it home over the years, including the 18th-century financier, John Law, who held high office at the Court of pre-revolution France, and William Robert Reid, proprietor of a prestigious firm of cabinet-makers in Edinburgh. The latter was an enthusiastic collector of antiques, fine furniture, prints and other works

gazetteer

of art, and he bought Lauriston Castle in 1902 to provide a suitable setting for his collections. In order to preserve their cherished home and its contents intact, Mr and Mrs Reid bequeathed the entire property to the nation in 1926.

The oldest part of the house, a tower-house which now forms the south-west corner of the building, dates back to the late 16th century and includes the lovely Oak Room; the remainder was added in two phases during the 19th century. The grounds are equally pleasant; telephone for details of special events.

Open all year by guided tour only; most days.

Antique furniture, collected at the turn of the century, adorns the house

 **gazetteer**

Palace of Holyroodhouse

(AT EAST END OF ROYAL MILE)

TEL: 0131 7371 & 0131 556 1096 (INFO)

A courtyard view of the magnificent Palace of Holyroodhouse

The Palace grew from the guesthouse of the Abbey of the Holyrood, said to have been founded by David I after a miraculous apparition. Mary, Queen of Scots, had her court here from 1561 to 1567, and 'Bonnie' Prince Charlie held levees at the Palace during his occupation of Edinburgh. The Palace is still used by the Royal Family, but can be visited when they are not in residence. Little remains of the original abbey except the ruined 13th-century nave of the church. The oldest part of the palace proper is James V's tower, with Mary's rooms on the second floor. A plaque marks the spot where the Italian courtier Rizzio was murdered. The audience chamber where she debated with John Knox can also be seen. There are fine 17th-century state rooms, and the picture gallery is notable for its series of Scottish monarchs, starting

in 330 BC with Fergus I. The work was done by Jacob de Wet in 1684–5; many of the likenesses are based on imagination. The grounds are used for royal garden parties in summer.

Open all year, daily.

Scotland's independent parliament last sat in 1707, in this 17th-century building now hidden behind an 1829 façade. It is now the seat of the Supreme Law Courts of Scotland and has been adapted to its changed use, but the Parliament Hall still has its fine old hammerbeam roof. A large stained glass window depicts the inauguration of the Court of Session in 1540.

Open all year, most days.

Parliament House
SUPREME COURT
TEL: 0131 225 2595

The museum, housed in the 16th-century tolbooth, tells the story of the ordinary people of Edinburgh from the late 18th century to the present day.

Reconstructions include a prison cell, 1930s pub and 1940s kitchen supported by photographs, displays, sounds, smells and a video.

Open all year, most days.

The People's Story
CANONGATE TOLBOOTH,
163 CANONGATE
TEL: 0131 225 2424 EXT
4057

The garden offers 70 acres (28ha) of peace and greenery close to the city centre. It was founded as a Physic Garden in 1670 at Holyrood and came to Inverleith in 1823. The largest rhodo-dendron collection in Britain can be seen here, and the different areas include an arboretum, a peat garden, a woodland garden, rock and heath gardens. There is a splendid herbaceous border, and the plant houses have orchids, cacti and other specialities from a variety of climates. The garden has colour all year round, even in winter when the plants with coloured bark come into their own.

The exhibition hall has informative displays, and Inverleith House Gallery holds regular art exhibitions. All major routes and areas of interest are accessible to wheelchairs, and there are purpose-built toilets for wheelchair users. Wheelchairs are also available at the entrance.

Open all year, daily. Closed 25 Dec & 1 Jan.

Royal Botanic Garden
INVERLEITH ROW (1M N)
TEL: 0131 552 7171

This magnificent museum houses extensive international collections covering the Decorative Arts, Natural History, Science, Technology and Working Life, and Geology. A lively programme of special events including temporary exhibitions, films, lectures and concerts takes place throughout the year.

Open all year, daily. Closed 25–26 Dec & 1–2 Jan.

Royal Museum of Scotland
CHAMBERS ST
TEL: 0131 225 7534

Royal Observatory Visitor Centre
BLACKFORD HILL
TEL: 0131 668 8405

The Visitor Centre explains the fascinating world of modern astronomy and the work of Scotland's national observatory. The main exhibition, 'The Universe', takes visitors on a tour of space and time from the present day Solar System to the beginning of it all. Models, 'hands-on' exhibits, videos, computer games and stunning deep-sky photographs explain the latest discoveries about the Universe in simple, everyday language. 'Reaching for the Stars' describes 100 years of work at the Royal Observatory; the 'Star Chamber' is an interactive discovery room where the science important to astronomy is explained. The Visitor Centre rooftop gives panoramic views over the city and the Braid Hills. There is a collection of telescopes and during the dark winter evenings two small telescopes on site are used to give guided visual tours of the night sky. To book a session at the telescopes, telephone the observatory.

Open all year, daily. Closed 25 Dec & 1 Jan.

Scotch Whisky Heritage Centre
354 CASTLEHILL (AT THE TOP OF THE ROYAL MILE, BESIDE EDINBURGH CASTLE)
TEL: 0131 220 0441

Located at the bottom of Castle Hill is a fascinating attraction where you can travel through time to discover the history of Scotland's most famous export – whisky! As you follow the whisky trail to the present day the sights, sounds and smells evoke a vivid and memorable picture of the secrets of whisky making and the importance of the Scottish climate. Enter the lives of the Highland crofters distilling whisky for their own consumption, and marvel at the technical advances that enable whisky production to be carried on today. An extra bonus is the free dram of Scotch whisky offered to every adult visitor.

Open daily. Closed 25 Dec.

Scottish National Gallery of Modern Art
BELFORD RD (IN THE WEST END OF EDINBURGH)
TEL: 0131 556 8921

This gallery houses Scotland's finest collection of 20th century paintings and graphic art, and includes works by Picasso, Matisse, Giacometti, Sickert and Hockney. It also houses an unrivalled collection of 20th-century Scottish art, from the Colourists right up to the contemporary scene. It also possesses German Expressionism and French Art within its international collection, and one of the most important Dada and Surrealist collections in the world.

Open all year, daily. Closed 25–26 Dec & 1–2 Jan.

Scottish National Portrait Gallery
1 QUEEN ST
TEL: 0131 556 8921

The collection housed within this striking red Victorian building provides a visual history of Scotland from the 16th century to the present day, told through the portraits of the people who shaped it: royals and rebels, poets and philosophers, heroes and villains. Among the most famous are Mary, Queen of Scots, and Ramsay's Sir Walter Scott. The building also houses the National Collection of Photography.

Open all year, daily. Closed 25–26 Dec & 1–2 Jan.

The museum is in Edinburgh Castle. Exhibitions include 'The Story of the Scottish Soldier' and 'For Your Freedom and Ours: Poland, Scotland and World War II'.
 Open all year, daily.

The former Church of St George (1811) was designed by Robert Reid in Greco-Roman style and is now the modern record branch of the Scottish Record Office. It houses the exhibition '800 Years of Scottish History', and the Search Room is available to researchers.
 Open most days. Closed certain BHs & part of Nov.

The Writers' Museum is situated in the historic Lady Stair's House which dates from 1622. It is now a museum housing various objects associated with Robert Burns, Sir Walter Scott and Robert Louis Stevenson. Temporary exhibitions are planned throughout the year.
 Open all year, most days.

Scottish United Services Museum
EDINBURGH CASTLE
TEL: 0131 225 7534

West Register House
CHARLOTTE SQUARE
TEL: 0131 535 1314

The Writers' Museum
LADY STAIR'S HOUSE, LADY STAIR'S CLOSE, LAWNMARKET
TEL: 0131 529 4901

The handsome interior of the Scottish National Portrait Gallery

INFORMATION

Distance
15 miles (24km) with 7 miles
(11km) off-road

Difficulty
Moderate

OS Map
Landranger 1:50,000 sheet 66
(Edinburgh & Midlothian)

Tourist Information
Musselburgh (summer only), tel:
0131 665 6597; Granada
Service Area off A1, Old
Craighall near Musselburgh, tel:
0131 653 6172

Cycle Shops/Hire
The New Bike Shop (hire),
Tollcross, Edinburgh, tel: 0131
228 6333

There are fine views of the Pentland and Lammermuir Hills as you travel the quiet roads and cycle paths of this fairly gentle route (there are only two short sections on main roads). Points of interest are the Inveresk Lodge Garden, Preston Tower and the Prestongrange Industrial Heritage Museum.

Refreshments
Pubs and cafés in Musselburgh,
including Luca's Café; The
Quayside Restaurant, Fisherrow;
summer teas and snacks at the
Prestongrange Industrial Heritage
Museum.

START
The ride starts at the Jewel Playing
Fields at the junction of
Duddingston Park South and the
Jewel, 4 miles (6.5km) to the east
of Edinburgh. Park carefully at the
side of the road. The Innocent

The River Esk flows through Musselburgh into the Firth of Forth

Cycle Path runs direct to this point from the Royal Commonwealth Pool in central Edinburgh, 2½ miles (4km) away.

DIRECTIONS

1. From the Jewel Playing Fields head south along Duddingston Park South. Pass under the railway bridge, and at the traffic lights at Niddrie Crossroads turn left. Turn right at the old church that is now the Craigmillar Arts Festival Centre on to Whitehill Road. Continue for 1 mile (1.5km), cross the railway at Millerhill Depot and then turn left on to the cycle path. Pass under the A1 by the subway and immediately turn right following the sign 'Fisherrow and Musselburgh Station'; continue to the station via the cycle gate.

2. By Musselburgh Station turn right on to the path signposted 'Monktonhall and River Esk Walkway'. After ½ mile (1km) pass through the railway tunnel and follow the path to the left for a short distance. Pass through a second railway tunnel and enter the Stoneybank Housing Estate, where you turn right, left and right to come out at the mini-roundabout on the B6415. Go straight on to Ferguson Drive, passing the Monktonhall Golf Clubhouse on your left. The road goes under the railway (bridge 27) and brings you to a footbridge over the River Esk. Cross the river and turn left along the track towards Inveresk and Musselburgh. After 1 mile (1.5km) turn right away from the river and go up the short hill into Inveresk. Turn right at the main road and

The Dovecot, Preston Tower Gardens

pass Inveresk Lodge Garden on the right.

3. Continue through Inveresk village; bear left at Crookston Road and go on to cross over the railway bridge (cycles and pedestrians only). This road eventually becomes a cycle path alongside the A1, for ½ mile (1km). On this section you should get a fine view of the white-painted Falside Castle, on the skyline ahead. At the junction with the A6094 turn left and head into Wallyford. On the far side of the village take the second exit on the roundabout, the B1361 to North Berwick.

4. Continue along the B1361 for

Crossing the River Esk

1½ miles (2.5km) to Prestonpans, and stay on the North Berwick Road until you come to the Doocot (dovecot) on the left. Turn left just after this and follow signs to Preston Tower and Garden, looking out for the fine Mercat Cross. The gardens at Preston Tower make an ideal picnic stop. (If you have time, you may like to visit the battle site of the 1745 Battle of Prestonpans, which is 1 mile (1.5km) along the North Berwick Road.)

5. From Preston Tower head back towards Edinburgh on the B1361 and turn right at the outskirts of Prestonpans along Prestongrange Road. On a clear day you will be able to see as far as the twin

peaks of East and West Lomond, and the three high-rise apartment blocks across the Fort at Kirkcaldy. At the coast road, the B1348, turn left and continue to the Prestongrange Industrial Heritage Museum.

6. Stay on this road, and just after

joining the main road (B1348) cross over on to the track at the entrance to the Levenhall Links Leisure Park. Follow this behind the houses and then between the race course and the Ash Lagoons. Stay beside the race course, and turn left by the boulders into the Goose Green housing scheme.

WHAT TO LOOK OUT FOR

Fisherrow developed independently of Musselburgh and it had strong trading links with the Netherlands in the 15th century. Look out for a Flemish influence in some of the older buildings of Fisherrow.

There are many freshwater wild flowers along the River Esk Cycle/Walkway, especially in May and June, and you will often see swans here too.

Levenhall Links Leisure Park hosts a good collection of ducks, geese and marsh birds. Also look out for seaside plants such as viper's bugloss and common rock rose.

Take the first turn on the right, to come out at the weir on the River Esk. You will see the footbridge to your left: cross this and carry straight on along New Street. Continue to Fisherrow Harbour, where you can buy fresh fish and stop for refreshment.

7. At the end of New Street join the A199 heading towards Edinburgh. Go straight on, and at the traffic lights at Eastfield bear left. At this point, look for the new cycle path leading off to the left, which will return you to your starting point at the Jewel.
If you prefer to stay on the road continue for 1 mile (1.5km) to the roundabout at the A1 where you should take the pavement on the left (this is dual use for cyclists and pedestrians); follow the cycle/walkway, passing B&Q

and its car park before taking the subway under the A1. Stay on the cycle path between the houses and the Niddrie Burn to return to the starting point at the Jewel.

PLACES OF INTEREST

Inveresk
This charming village is now properly a suburb of Musselburgh, but nevertheless retains its own distinctive character. Extensive Roman remains have been found here, but it is the Georgian period which has left its mark on the village.
(See also page 53.)

Prestongrange Industrial Heritage Museum
The site, the oldest documented coal mine in Britain, is dominated

by the giant beam engine, which was originally used to pump out mine workings and was in use until 1954. The main exhibits are out of doors and can be viewed when the museum is closed.
(See also page 76.)

Prestonpans
Prestonpans gained its name from the salt pans, constructed here in the 12th century by monks from Newbattle Abbey.
(See also page 76.)

Musselburgh
As the harbour suggests, fishing was the main industry of this town which is named after a mussel bed at the river mouth.
(See also page 67.)

Passing pantiled cottages, Fisherrow

ETTRICK
VILLAGE OFF B709, 15 MILES (24KM) W OF HAWICK

EYEMOUTH
TOWN OFF A1107, 8 MILES (13KM) NW OF BERWICK-UPON-TWEED

Eyemouth Museum
AULD KIRK, MARKET PLACE
TEL: 018907 50678

This tiny hamlet is in Ettrick Forest, once heavily wooded but now sheep country. In the churchyard lies James Hogg, 'The Ettrick Shepherd', an important 19th-century poet and novelist. To the east of the church stands the Hogg monument, on the site of the former cottage where he was born in 1770.

A busy little fishing town and resort, on the Eye Water, where it flows into the sea between Hare Point and Nestends, Eyemouth is picturesquely situated. The jagged Hurkers rocks protect the harbour, and the beach is partly sandy, with bathing. Eyemouth was granted free port charter in 1597. It was renowned as a smuggling centre in the 1700s with secret passages all over town; Robert Adam's Gunsgreen House was at the centre of this. Along the coast are caves and caverns once used for smuggling, and at Hare Point are the remains of a fort.

The museum was opened in 1981 as a memorial to the 129 local fishermen lost in the Great Fishing Disaster of 1881. Its main feature is the 15-ft (4.5-m) tapestry, which was made for the centenary. There are also displays on local history, and temporary exhibitions.
Open Apr–Sep, daily.

Floors Castle is enormous – indeed, it is the largest inhabited house in Scotland. It was built in the early 18th century for the 1st Duke of Roxburghe, who played a leading part in the union of Scotland with England in 1707. Doubtless the situation of his home in the Borders coloured his views, for this was a troubled frontier of cross-border skirmishes and moving boundaries for many centuries before the two countries united.

The castle's architect was William Adam, but his creation was enlarged and embellished about a century later by William Playfair, whose many other commissions included the National Gallery in Edinburgh. It was he who added the countless pepper-pot cupolas which give Floors its fairy-tale appearance today. By this time the 6th Duke was in residence, having inherited the title and the estate at the age of just seven years. He was the heir of Sir James Innes, who had won the inheritance after a protracted and very expensive court case during which a number of distant relatives claimed the dukedom. Sir James was 76 years old and childless when he was granted the title and the estate, encouraging many of his unsuccessful rivals to wait eagerly in the wings for a second chance. However, in his 80s he fathered a son, James – the 6th Duke. James both increased the family fortunes and its importance to such an extent that he was honoured

FLOORS CASTLE
(1 MILE/1.5KM N OF KELSO)
TEL: 01573 223333

The largest inhabited mansion in Scotland, Floors Castle is set in pleasant gardens above the River Tweed

Floors Castle was seen world-wide when it appeared as the ancestral home of Tarzan in the film Greystoke

'...altogether a kingdom Oberon and Titania to dwell in.'
Sir Walter Scott

with a state visit from Queen Victoria in 1867 – a summer-house in the garden was built especially for her.

Though the exterior of the castle has changed little since the 6th Duke's day, the interior was considerably altered by the 8th Duke around the turn of the century. For the contents we must largely thank his wife, the American heiress Mary Goelet, who devoted herself to the house she had been taken to as a bride in 1903. From her Long Island home she brought the wonderful collection of 17th-century Brussels tapestries which adorn the walls of Floors Castle, and she also acquired the collections of French furniture and contemporary art which enhance the elegant rooms here. The Needle Room, reputedly identical to a room at Versailles, now acts as a gallery for paintings by Matisse, Redon, Bonnard and Augustus John.

The gardens and grounds around Floors Castle are delightful; they contain a holly tree which is said to mark the spot where James II was killed whilst besieging the castle.

Open Etr–Sep, daily; Oct, certain days.

(See also Kelso, page 60.)

These two bridges cross the Firth of Forth 9 miles (14.5km) west of Edinburgh. The Forth road bridge was opened in 1964, a graceful suspension bridge carrying the A90 2,000yds (1,828m) over the Firth, one of the world's largest suspension bridges. The Forth railway bridge was completed in 1890; a double rail-line runs through the stone approach viaducts to the cantilevered steel bridge with three towers.

FORTH BRIDGES
BRIDGES CARRYING A90 AND RAILWAY

The Forth railway bridge

INFORMATION

Total Distance
24 miles (38.5km)

Difficulty
Challenging

OS Map
Landranger 1:50,000 sheet 66
(Edinburgh & Midlothian)

Tourist Information
Dalkeith, tel: 0131 663
2083/660 6818

Cycle Shops/Hire
Dalkeith Bike Shed, Dalkeith, tel:
0131 654 1170; The New Bike
Shop Tollcross, Edinburgh (hire),
tel: 0131 228 6333

Refreshments
Emmaus Tea Room, Main Street,
Pathhead, open all day. Vogrie
Country Park, cafeteria. The
Scottish Mining Museum, open
April to September. Cavaliere
Restaurant, High Street, Dalkeith.
County Restaurant, High Street,
Dalkeith. Continental Café, Jarnac
Court, Dalkeith. Excellent picnic
areas in Vogrie Country Park and
at Crichton Castle. There are
picnic tables at the Scottish
Mining Museum, Newtongrange.

The early stages of this ride offer marvellous views of the Forth and Berwick Law. You then proceed across a ford to enjoy the Pentland Hills, and pause in the popular Vogrie Country Park; there is also the opportunity to visit the Scottish Mining Museum. The route includes three short steep sections which are easily walked if preferred.

A cyclist enjoys a shaded ride in Vogrie Country Park

Cycle ride

START

Dalkeith is just 10 miles (16km) south-east of Edinburgh on the A68, and the starting point of the ride is Dalkeith Country Park at the north-east end of the High Street (A6094) by St Mary's Church.

DIRECTIONS

1. Turn left from the car park following the sign to Whitecraig and Musselburgh (A6094) and at the roundabout, take the second exit towards Thorney Bank Industrial Estate (B6414). Turn left, still on the B6414, towards Tranent. You will soon be on your first real hill of the ride but it quickly levels out as you reach the cottages and then a junction where you carry straight on. At the next crossroads carry straight on to Cousland (another short hill) and pass through the village of pretty cottages. After 2 miles (3km) turn right at the T-junction (not signed) and follow the road for a further 1 mile (1.5km) to reach the main A6093.

2. Turn left on to the A6093, then soon right, signposted 'Pathhead (B6367)'. Take the first left, continue for 650 yards (600m) then turn right on to the B6371. Continue for 3¼ miles (5km) then turn right at a minor road, signed 'Windy Mains'. You really are off the beaten track now as you pass the Saw Mill and then cross the ford at the Salters Burn – there is a bridge if the water is high. (You could also walk the 55yards/50m up the hill out of the ford.) Look for the pheasant farm on your left and a white dovecot in the distance on your right, with Whitburgh House beyond. At the next junction turn left then almost immediately right for 550 yards (500m) to emerge at a slightly off-set crossroads; go straight on until you reach the A68. Turn right and stay on the A68 for 270 yards (250m), then turn left on to the B6458, signed 'Tynehead' (there is a pavement on this section where it is possible to walk your cycle).

3. Continue along the B6458 for 2½ miles (4km) to reach Tynehead where you turn right by the telephone box following the sign to Crichton Castle. At Crichton village turn left and then right at the telephone box, signed 'Pathhead'. (To visit the castle follow the signs from the village.) Continue along the B6367 to Pathhead, where there are shops, the Emmaus Tea Room and a village pub.

Outside the Scottish Mining Museum in Newton Grange

Inside the Scottish Mining Museum at Newtongrange – the steam winding engine

4. From Pathhead take the minor road, signed 'Ford and Edgehead' for almost 1 mile (1.5km) before turning left on the B6372, signed 'Dewartown, Newlandrig and Gorebridge'. Go through Dewartown to reach Vogrie Country Park; this would be an ideal picnic stop. Carry on for a further 2 miles (3km), turn right and carry straight on following the Newtongrange sign. Turn right at a T-junction after 1 mile (1.5km) and right again at the next T-junction to see the

Scottish Mining Museum.
5. From the museum continue downhill and turn right after 330 yards (300m), signed 'Easthouses'. Continue through Newtongrange, going straight on at the crossroads and past Newbattle Abbey before coming to the roundabout at Eskbank Toll where you take the A6094 into Dalkeith. Keep going straight on at each junction to return to Dalkeith Country Park.

PLACES OF INTEREST

Dalkeith Country Park
Although part of the Duke of Buccleuch's estate, Dalkeith

House (not open), dating back 700 years, is no longer a ducal seat. The park has nature trails and forests, walks along the River Esk, a woodland playground considered to be one of the best in Scotland, and Dalkeith Old Wood contains oak trees over 300 years old. Just inside the gateway to the park is St Mary's Church, which was built as the palace chapel. It is open on Saturdays and Sundays and teas are served in July and August.

Vogrie Country Park
This is a typical 19th-century estate with a formalised park, farmland and woods. A

42

refreshment room and an adventure playground make this an ideal picnic spot all year round.

Crichton Castle

Situated on the banks of the Tyne near Crichton village, the 14th- to 16th-century buildings of this Historic Scotland property include a fine Italianate arcade by the Earl of Bothwell. The castle is open from April to September.
(See also page 9.)

WHAT TO LOOK OUT FOR

In April and May there is a fine display of spring flowers on many parts of the route, but particularly in Crichton and in the window boxes of Dewartown village. The entrance to Newbattle Abbey has an impressive stone gateway well worth a photograph. The village of Tynehead is the source of the River Tyne that flows right across East Lothian through the country town of Haddington, eventually reaching the sea at Tynemouth by Dunbar. Roe deer, squirrels and many water birds can be seen in Dalkeith Country Park, and the Montagu Bridge built by Adam about 1792 is also a feature of the park.

The Scottish Mining Museum:

This exhibition has been established at the Lady Victoria colliery in Newtongrange. Visitors can experience life in a coal- mining family in this realistic presentation, after being issued with a helmet and token to meet mining regulations! There is also a shop and café. The museum is open April to October.
(See also page 68.)

Relax for a while at the Vogrie Country Park

GALASHIELS
Town on A7, 12 miles (19km) N of Hawick

This industrial Border town on Gala Water has been famous since the 18th century for woollen textiles, especially for tweeds and hosiery. The College of Textiles and various mills are open to the public. The Mercat Cross dates from 1695, and the town crest, with its motto 'Sour Plums', as depicted on the Municipal Buildings, recalls the deaths of some English soldiers in a Border foray of 1337, after gathering plums. An old track, known as the 'Catrail', or Pict's Ditch, passes westwards of the town on high ground, and is thought to have extended for more than 50 miles (80.5km) in a southerly direction.

GARVALD
Village off B6370, 8 miles (13km) SW of Dunbar

A tiny village in the Lammermuirs, with a partly 12th-century church. Near by is Nunraw Abbey, abandoned after the Reformation and revived by Cistercians in 1946.

GIFFORD
Village on B6369, 4 miles (6km) S of Haddington

This delightful 18th-century estate village with a contemporary church and a wide main street, is situated on the Gifford Water, with views to the south of the Lammermuir Hills. Yester House is a fine Adam mansion dating from 1745. Beyond it lie the remains of Yester Castle with its remarkable 13th-century underground hall known as 'Goblin Ha'.

GORDON
Village on A6089, 8 miles (13km) NW of Kelso

A small village north of Mellerstain House, a fine Adam mansion with terraced gardens. The 16th-century L-plan Greenknow Tower lies to the north.

Mellerstain House
(5 miles/8km E of Earlston, on unclassified road)
Tel: 01573 410225

This grand and imposing mansion, home of the Earl and Countess of Haddington, was built in two stages – the first by William Adam in 1725 and the second by his more famous son, Robert, in the 1770s.

Although the house is 18th-century through and through, the ancestors of the current Earl and Countess, the Baillies, had owned the estate since 1642. Mixed fortunes in the early years led various members of the family into imprisonment, exile and execution. However, a young and penniless George Baillie fled to

Holland to become a junior officer in the Prince of Orange's Horse Guards. When the same Prince of Orange became William III of England, the family fortunes were restored so they were in a position to create this beautiful home, which has been splendidly preserved in its original style.

The classical interiors are among the finest you will see anywhere – the library has justifiably been hailed as a masterpiece – and the intricate plaster ceilings and panels are exquisite. Elegant furniture and fine paintings more than adequately set off the design and decoration of each of the rooms, and as well as many family portraits the house contains works by Van Dyck, Gainsborough, Ramsay, Aikman and Nasmyth.

Open Etr–Sep, certain days.

Mellerstain House, seen from the parterre

On the north bank of the Tweed, just to the east of the Royal Burgh of Peebles, the Glentress picnic areas provide a choice of secluded spots with lovely views overlooking small ponds, or across the Tweed Valley at the higher sites. There are many waymarked walks, mountain bike trails and pony treks in the forest.

HOW TO GET THERE

Head east out of Peebles on the A72. The Falla Brae car park and picnic area is signposted 1 mile (1.5km) in advance; a small track off to the left leads to the car park and on to other sites within the forest.

FACILITIES

Ample car parking (small charge), with picnic tables and benches.
Toilets.
Information boards.
Marked trails and guided walks arranged by Lothian and Tweed Forest District Forest Enterprise.

Glentress is the oldest of the Forest Enterprise forests in the Borders, with plantings dating back to 1920. It rises to a height of 1,968 feet (600m) above the valley floor and the various waymarked walks give ample opportunity to enjoy wonderful views of the Tweed Valley. The predominant tree species is spruce, but there are also larch, pine and a variety of deciduous, broadleaf species. Wildlife is abundant in the area, with over 80 species of bird having been recorded; the visitor may be fortunate enough to spot some of the more elusive animals such as roe deer, badger, foxes and red squirrels.

Peebles

A royal burgh since the reign of David I, Peebles boasts a number of antiquities which have survived the area's turbulent history. Neidpath Castle, perched above a bend in the Tweed about 1 mile (1.5km) to the west of Peebles, is a fine example of a medieval tower house, with 17th-century additions. There are good views from the top.

(See also page 70.)

Traquair House dates from the 12th century

Traquair House

Traquair House, on the south bank of the Tweed, is reached by turning off the A72 in Innerleithen onto the B709. It is the oldest inhabited house in Scotland.

(See also page 85.)

GETTING ABOUT

Those who do not wish to walk through the woods can hire mountain bikes or even go pony trekking.

GOREBRIDGE
TOWN OFF A7, 4 MILES (6.5KM) S OF DALKEITH

A small town near which stands the Palladian mansion of Arniston House, the Dundas family seat.

Arniston House
TEL: 01875 830238

This fine William Adam mansion was commissioned in 1725 by Robert Dundas; it was finished in the 1750s by William's son John Adam. The Dundas family were already established landowners in Scotland when Robert Dundas became Lord President of the Court of Session. The house contains portraits of the various generations from the 16th century up to the present day, including works by Ramsay and Raeburn. The present owners, the Dundas-Bekker family, are undergoing a lengthy programme of restoration work on the house. The John Adam dining room ruined by dry rot in the 1950s has been successfully restored and is now open to the public. As much public access as possible is made available.

Open Jul–mid Sep, certain days.

GREENLAW
VILLAGE ON A6105, 7 MILES (11KM) SW OF DUNS

Once the county town of Berwickshire, until replaced by Duns, Greenlaw lies on the upper reaches of Blackadder Water. It takes its name from a low 'green law', or isolated hill. Its 18th-century church tower was built in the style of the late 15th century, for use as a prison. A few miles south is the ruined Hume Castle, at a height of some 600ft (183m), having been captured by Cromwell in 1651, and to a certain extent restored in 1794. The castle makes a good viewpoint.

GULLANE
VILLAGE ON A198, 3¾ MILES (6KM) W OF NORTH BERWICK

This pretty coastal village on the Firth of Forth has dunes, beaches and fine views. Parts of the old church are Norman. Muirfield championship golf course is near by.

HADDINGTON
TOWN ON A1, 16 MILES (25.5KM) E OF EDINBURGH

Once an important trading town, the lovely royal burgh of Haddington was besieged and burnt three times by the English during the Middle Ages. It has over 130 buildings listed as being of important historical or architectural interest. The unusually shaped market square is divided by the Town House, designed in 1748 by William Adam, and Sidgate contains Haddington House (1680). The late medieval Church of St Mary the Virgin dates from 1462; it was damaged during an English siege in 1548 and finally restored in the 1970s. The Lauderdale Aisle includes Elizabethan alabaster monuments and the tomb of Jane Welsh Carlyle, wife of the historian, who was born here. Haddington was also the birthplace of Alexander II and possibly of John Knox. South of the town lies Lennoxlove House, seat of the Dukes of Hamilton. Mainly dating from the 17th century, it has Mary Stuart connections and a fine interior.

*S*easide walks are always fun and this one is no exception. It goes along an excellent sandy beach beside the broad Firth of Forth and returns beside the famous Muirfield golf course.

Grid ref: NT476831
INFORMATION
The walk is 2½ miles (4km) long. Good paths, but soft going across the sand dunes.

Dogs can run on the beach, but should be kept on leads by the golf course.

Pubs and cafés in Gullane. Toilets near the car park.

The dunes at Gullane Bay

START
Gullane is 15 miles (24km) east of Edinburgh. Turn off the A198 in Gullane at the sign 'To the Beach' and park at Gullane Bents car park.

DIRECTIONS
From the car park walk down the tarmac path to the beach, reached by a gap through the dunes. There is a play area to the left.

Turn right and walk along the beach on the firm sand. The view extends from Edinburgh over to the Fife Hills and round towards the Bass Rock.

When you reach the rocks go up to the right and walk along the shore path, passing concrete blocks placed here in World War II as tank traps, then over a shingle beach. The path goes through the dunes (soft sand and harder going) then improves to run outside a fence to reach the scant remains of an old chapel.

The path winds inland following the line of a stone dyke. Continue up a broad grassy path, keeping the wood on your right. The path swings right to start the return journey, passing

GULLANE BAY

along the edge of Muirfield golf course. Pass through a fence beside a gate (note the warning about keeping dogs under close control because of rabbit snares).

Cross the end of the road over the golf course and pass to the right of a green shed. Turn left at a wooden gatepost and continue with the fence on your left. At a junction fork left, at the next junction go left, and at an open area head for a signpost about 50yds (46m) ahead. Turn right on a broad grass path to wind through the dunes and return to the beach.

Gullane Bents

Considerable work has gone on here to restore the dune system, which suffered in the 1920s and '30s from vehicles being driven down to the beach, and between 1941–5 from military training – the area was used as a practice ground for the Normandy invasion in 1944.

Information boards give details of how the restoration has taken place.

Muirfield Golf Course

Muirfield is one of the famous 'links' courses on which the British Open is played, when the world's best golfers pit their skills against the natural hollows, knolls and traps.

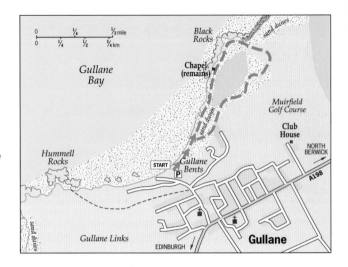

WHAT TO LOOK OUT FOR

This is a superb area for nature study. Over 200 species of birds have been recorded here and at Aberlady Bay to the west, including many waders and seabirds. In winter thousands of common and velvet scoters and brent geese are seen. The area is also rich in interesting plants including autumn gentian, burnet rose and northern marsh orchids. Grey and common seals are often seen offshore, especially near the Hummell Rocks, at the west end of Gullane Bay.

The course at Muirfield

Aircraft on display include a Supermarine Spitfire MK 16, De Haviland Sea Venom, Hawker Sea Hawk and Comet (4). The museum is set out in a former airship base, and also has a section on Airship R34 which flew from here to New York and back in 1919. There is also an extensive display of rockets and aero-engines.
   Open Etr–Sep, daily.

Museum of Flight
East Fortune Airfield (Signposted from A1 near Haddington)
Tel: 01620 880308 or 0131 225 7534

Pronounced 'Hoyk', this is a centre of the knitwear industry and largest of the Border towns, largely rebuilt after a fire in 1570. One of the few buildings to survive the fire was Drumlanrig's Tower, which became a hotel. Anne, the widow of the executed Duke of Monmouth, and with whom Sir Walter Scott's *Lay of the Last Minstrel* is associated, lived here once. An attractive town with good tourist facilities, Hawick is noted for its Common Riding, held each June. Horsemen ride the town's marches or boundaries to commemorate the local teenagers who rallied to defeat marauding English troops in 1514. This was a year after Flodden, when practically all the men of Hawick were wiped out. The Horse Monument in the High Street records the event.

HAWICK
Town on A7, 11 miles (17.5km) S of Selkirk

Drumlanrig's Tower has a fascinating history, beginning in its earliest years when the Tower served as a fortified keep in the 12th century – occupied by the Black Douglas of Drumlanrig; through to a more genteel age in the 18th century when Anne, Duchess of Monmouth and Buccleuch transformed it into a glittering residence. Later the Tower served as a gracious hotel. It has now been transformed into a major visitor attraction with historic room setting, costumed figures, dioramas, sounds, smells and audio visual programmes. Many events are planned throughout the year.
   Open all year, daily.

Drumlanrig's Tower
Tower Knowe
Tel: 01450 373457

Wilton Lodge Park forms a beautiful setting for this museum on the history, trades and wildlife of the Borders. There is an interesting range of exhibitions throughout the year, and the park has riverside walks and gardens. There are displays on the history of Hawick's hosiery and knitwear trade, Hawick Common Riding and the town's sporting associations.
   Open all year, daily.

Hawick Museum and Scott Gallery
Wilton Lodge Park (¾ mile/1km W from High St, following river)
Tel: 01450 373457

This upland village is sited high up in the Moorfoot Hills on the main Carlisle–Edinburgh road. Heriot Water is a tributary of the Tweed; rolling grassy heathland surrounds it.

HERIOT
Village on B709, 7 miles (11km) NW of Stow

HERMITAGE CASTLE

Site off B6399, 5 miles (8km) N of Newcastleton

Tel: 0131 668 8800

The river that runs near the castle is known as Hermitage Water. Some 600 feet (183m) away from the castle, on the banks of the river, stand the remains of the medieval hermitage which gave Hermitage Castle its name.

Great walls of dark sandstone loom menacingly across the Borders, and Sir Walter Scott noted that even in his time the local people regarded this brooding fortress 'with peculiar aversion and terror'.

The merest glance explains why, for the walls rise sheer and imposing from among the grassy earthworks, and windows are few and far between. The only significant openings are the rows of doors on the very top part of the castle, which afforded access to the wooden fighting balcony that once protruded from the walls. The tower was developed from a simple 13th-century rectangular building to the grim fortress that can be seen today, by the Douglas family in the late 14th century. One of the two great flying arches was reconstructed in the 19th century, but, all in all, Hermitage appears much as it would have done in the 15th century.

Several of Hermitage's owners committed foul deeds within its walls. One drowned a colleague near the castle, but was later boiled alive for his misdeeds, which included witchcraft. Another starved his enemies to death in the pit dungeons, although he too met an unpleasant end, murdered in a nearby forest. And Hermitage was also where Mary, Queen of Scots rushed to be at the bedside of her ailing lover, the Earl of Bothwell.

Open Apr–Sep, daily; Oct–Mar, certain days. Closed 25–26 Dec & 1–2 Jan.

Its lonely setting and violent past give Hermitage Castle an eerie atmosphere

A village at the foot of the Lammermuir Hills, noted for the Children's Village, a charitable institution founded in 1886 for disabled children in Edinburgh.

HUMBIE
VILLAGE ON B6368, 8 MILES (13KM) SW OF HADDINGTON

Hume Castle, seat of the Homes from 1214 to 1611 and demolished by Cromwell's troops in 1650, stands near the village. There are magnificent views all around.

HUME
VILLAGE OFF B6364, 3 MILES (5KM) S OF GREENLAW

This permanent showground and home of the Royal Highland Show since 1960, is in the grounds of Ingliston House (1846). There is a large Sunday market and motor-racing near by.

INGLISTON
SHOWGROUND OFF M8, 7 MILES (11KM) W OF EDINBURGH

A fascinating collection illustrating rural Scotland through the ages: the tools and equipment, the workers and their families. Visitors can see the oldest threshing mill in the world, models of the first reaping machines, numerous photographs, interesting folk art and a range of excellent audio-visual presentations.
Open all year, daily. Closed Xmas & New Year.

Scottish Agricultural Museum
(AT EAST GATE OF ROYAL HIGHLAND SHOWGROUND)
TEL: 0131 333 2674

This famous tweed and knitwear centre on the River Tweed is noted for cashmere and lambswool. It became a spa town in the 19th century and its mineral springs are still open. Sir Walter Scott used the town as inspiration for St Ronan's Well in his eponymous novel. There are numerous hill-forts in the vicinity. Northwards lie the Leithen Water and Glentress Water valleys, in a delightful setting of hills. To the south of Innerleithen, across the Tweed, is situated the famous old mansion of Traquair House.
(See also page 85.)

INNERLEITHEN
SMALL TOWN ON A72, 6 MILES (10KM) SE OF PEEBLES

These buildings contain a Victorian office, a paper store with reconstructed waterwheel, a composing room and a press room. The machinery is in full working order and visitors may view the printer at work and have 'hands-on' experience in typesetting in the composing room.
Open May–Sep, daily; Oct, certain days.

Robert Smail's Printing Works
7/9 HIGH ST
TEL: 01896 830206

Pleasantly situated on the River Esk, this attractive residential village, now a suburb of Musselburgh, was developed for Edinburgh merchants in the early 18th century. It was once a Roman station, numerous remains having been excavated. The parish church is set on a height; it replaced an older church in 1805, and has a tall spire and an exceptionally lovely churchyard.

INVERESK
SUBURB IMMEDIATELY S OF MUSSELBURGH

Inveresk Lodge Garden
(A6124 S OF MUSSELBURGH)
TEL: 0131 665 1855

With a good deal of appeal, this charming terraced garden specialises in plants, shrubs and roses suitable for growing on small plots. The 17th-century house makes an elegant backdrop.

Open all year, most days.

(See also Cycle ride: A Circuit East of Edinburgh, page 32.)

JEDBURGH
TOWN ON B6358, 10 MILES (16KM) NE OF HAWICK

Once a quintessential Border fortress town, with a fortified castle and abbey, Jedburgh stands on the Jed Water near the Cheviot Hills. The castle was destroyed in 1409 and the town is now noted for the remains of Jedburgh Abbey, founded as a priory by David I in 1138. The abbey and monastic buildings formed a large complex, but from the late 13th century this was continuously damaged, and the monastery was closed in 1560 during the Reformation. The abbey church then became the parish kirk and is well preserved, with a lovely, richly-carved Norman west door, a fine rose window known as St Catherine's Wheel, a lofty nave with transitional Norman-Gothic architectural details and a 12th-century arched and pillared choir.

The town has a charming little market place and the crow-stepped, gabled Mary Queen of Scots House, where Mary Stuart once stayed. There are many houses displaying characteristic crow-stepped gables, and Jedburgh is one of the most attractive towns in the Lowlands. There is a Riding in July into the attractive surrounding countryside.

Jeddart Handba' was a local ball game, said to originate when local men returned from the Border raids and played ball with the heads of their English victims.

Jedburgh Abbey
4–5 ABBEY BRIDGEND
TEL: 0131 668 8800

Standing as the most complete of the Border monasteries, although it has been sacked and rebuilt many times, Jedburgh Abbey has been described as 'the most perfect and beautiful example of the Saxon and early

Gothic in Scotland'. Remains of some of the domestic buildings have been uncovered during excavations.

Open all year, daily. Closed 25–26 Dec & 1–3 Jan.

Mary, Queen of Scots visited Jedburgh in 1556, and had to prolong her stay because of ill-health. This splendid house is now a museum devoted to her memory and tragic history. An unusual feature of this 16th-century fortified dwelling is the left-handed spiralling staircase: the Kers, the owners of the house, were left-handed and the special staircase allowed the men to use their sword hands. The museum presents a thought-provoking interpretation of Mary, Queen of Scots' tragic life with period rooms, stunning murals and personal items connected with her.

Open Mar–Nov, daily.

Mary Queen of Scots House
QUEEN ST
TEL: 01835 863331

The attractive Jedburgh Abbey with its Visitor Centre obelisk

*T*his is a satisfying walk through mature woodlands and along the quiet River Teviot and is one of four colour-coded walks ranging in length. Various attractions include a historic dovecote, a clock tower and a fine Visitor Centre.

At the woodland centre

Grid ref: NT649247

INFORMATION
The walk is 2½ miles (4km) long.
No road walking.
A few stiles.
Shop and tearoom at Visitor Centre.

START
The Harestanes Visitor Centre is at Monteviot, 3 miles (5km) north of Jedburgh at the junction of the A68 and B6400. Start at the courtyard at the rear of the centre.

DIRECTIONS
This walk is one marked with blue waymarkers and is called 'The Doocot Walk'. Follow the path alongside the entrance drive past estate sawmills. Turn right at the top of the drive, through mixed woodland, past the old cricket pavilion towards the footbridge. Turn right and cross the footbridge over the Marble Burn. Continue until the paths divide, turning left and keeping to the path near the edge of the wood. At the tarmac drive enter the woodland opposite by bearing left when crossing the drive. Turn right and follow a track across a stile and along the edge of the field. To your right along this path you will see the clock tower of the old stables. On reaching the woodland at the riverside, turn left and follow the path past the Doocot and over the old mill lade to the viewing platform on the River Teviot (view of Monteviot Suspension Bridge).

Walk

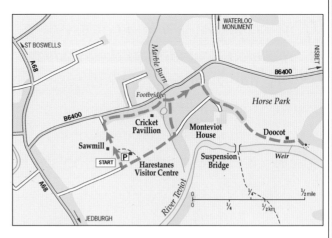

Retrace your steps to the Marble Burn and go straight on, passing the pond on your right. The path then leaves the track and leads down to the burn. Turn right to walk alongside the tarmac track towards the Visitor Centre (look out for traffic near buildings). At the road junction turn right to return to the start point.

The Waterloo Monument

The Waterloo Monument stands on Peniel Heugh, the site of an Iron Age fort. It is dedicated to the Duke of Wellington and the British Army and was erected in 1815 by the sixth Marquis of Lothian. The tower collapsed in the following year, and its replacement was eventually capped in timber in 1867. The wooden top is now rotting and, therefore, unsafe.

The historic dovecote

WHAT TO LOOK OUT FOR

The theme of the centre, based on the old home farm of a large country estate, is the use of wood. Needless to say, the woodland contains many species, both native and introduced. Next to the old mill lade on the River Teviot there is a magnificent purpose-built viewing platform, from where you can observe the area's many birds such as coal tits, buzzards and jackdaws. The line of Dere Street, the old Roman Road from Newsteads to Corbridge, can be seen beyond the river.

The Doocot

Pigeons, or 'doos', used to be a valuable source of food in times of scarcity, and they were bred by landowners from the 16th century onwards in doocots (dovecotes). The doocot on this walk stands on a rise to the left of the path next to the river. The lower part dates from the 17th-century. It is about 20 feet (6m) in diameter and is lined inside with stone nesting-boxes for hundreds of pigeons. Because it is in a dangerous condition, the doocot is not accessible to the public.

JOHN MUIR COUNTRY PARK

*T*he picnic site is a large grassy area, sheltered behind sand dunes which hide the fine view out over Belhaven Bay. Looking out from the dunes on a clear day, the impressive mass of the Bass Rock rises out of the sea. The site is well serviced, with an adventure play area that includes climbing frames, and a number of waymarked walks.

The Bass Rock at sunset

HOW TO GET THERE

Head south from Edinburgh on the A1, and follow the signs to Dunbar, taking the A1087 at the roundabout. Just before the sign for West Barns take the small track off to the left, signposted to John Muir Country Park.

FACILITIES

Ample car parking.
Toilets, with access for disabled people.
Picnic tables, benches, litter bins and an extensive children's play area.
Information panels and leaflets.

In 1831 John Muir and his parents emigrated from Dunbar to

JOHN MUIR COUNTRY PARK

the United States, where he became a pioneer of conservation and was instrumental in establishing the National Parks scheme. The country park covers 1,648 acres (667ha) with a variety of habitats including sandy and rocky shores, cliffs, sand dunes, saltmarsh and woodland. A wide range of wildlife includes over 400 species of plant and exceptional numbers of various waders and wildfowl, especially during winter. There are a number of waymarked walks and bridleways which pass through the park. The sand dunes form a welcome windbreak against the raw easterly winds which blow in off the North Sea.

DUNBAR

The royal burgh of Dunbar dates from 1455, and Dunbar Castle, now a fragmented ruin, has a long and auspicious history stretching back to 1338 when Black Agnes, Countess of Dunbar, defended it against a 19-week siege by the Earl of Salisbury. Mary, Queen of Scots later took refuge here twice, resulting in the order for the castle's destruction. Dunbar first prospered as a herring fishing port in the early 18th century, and later as a whaling port, with boats sailing as far as the Arctic. Dunbar is still a delightful town.

CLOSE BY

Tyninghame is a good example of an estate village constructed at the beginning of the 19th century, and has many well preserved buildings. East Linton has fine pubs and interesting shops; nearby Preston Mill has been restored to full working order by the National Trust for Scotland. Hailes Castle lies in the shadow of Traprain Law, with its Bronze Age and Roman remains. Set on the banks of the River Tyne, the castle is another reminder of Scotland's stormy past.

(See also pages 16, 82, 83 & 89.)

Preston Mill, now restored to full working order

KELSO
TOWN ON A698, 8 MILES (13KM) SW OF COLDSTREAM

Set on the confluence of the rivers Teviot and Tweed, Kelso is the site of the remains of a 12th-century abbey, once Scotland's most powerful, destroyed in 1545. The attractive town has a wide market place, and has many historical attractions, including visits from Mary, Queen of Scots and Prince Charles Edward. Sir Walter Scott lived here for six months, in 1783, as a pupil at the former grammar school, staying at Garden Cottage, now Waverley Lodge. At the same school were the brothers Ballantyne, who later printed and published his works. In an impressive park west of the town is Floors Castle, a huge crenellated mansion.

(See also page 37.)

Kelso Abbey
TEL: 0131 668 8800

Founded by David I in 1128 and probably the greatest of the four famous Border abbeys, Kelso became extremely wealthy and acquired extensive lands. In 1545 it served as a fortress when the town was attacked by the Earl of Hertford, but now only fragments of the once-imposing abbey church give any clue to its long history.

Open at any reasonable time.

Kelso Museum
TURRET HOUSE, ABBEY COURT
TEL: 01573 225470

Kelso Museum reflects the life and times of this lively market town, going back to prehistoric beginnings and looking at its growth since the establishment of the Abbey in the 12th century. A Victorian schoolroom, a market scene and the interior of a skinner's workshop are popular features.

Open Etr–Oct, daily.

KIRK YETHOLM
VILLAGE ON B6352, 7 MILES (11KM) SE OF KELSO

The village is twinned with Town Yetholm, across Bowmount Water, near the English border. It was the headquarters of Scottish gypsies until the 1880s, when the last 'Queen' was buried here.

LADYKIRK
VILLAGE ON B6470, 6 MILES (9.5KM) NE OF COLDSTREAM

This village was named after a stone church dedicated to the Virgin Mary, built by James IV in 1499 after his escape from drowning while crossing a River Tweed ford. The present bridge was built in 1839. On the Northumberland side of the river is the ruined Norham Castle.

LAUDER
SMALL TOWN ON A68, 9 MILES (14.5KM) N OF MELROSE

A royal burgh and market town in Lauderdale with some fine buildings, including an impressive 18th-century town hall and cruciform church dating from the 1670s. In 1482 several favourites of James III were hanged from the former Lauder Bridge by the Earl of Angus, who earned for himself the sobriquet of 'Bell-the-Cat'.

Lauder's position on the Leader Water makes it a good angling centre. Outside the town is the park of Thirlestane Castle, with its castellated sandstone towers.

This fairy-tale castle has been the home of the Maitland family, the Earls of Lauderdale, since the 12th century, and some of the family still live in one of the wings. Some of the most splendid plasterwork ceilings in Britain may be seen in the 17th-century staterooms. The former family nurseries now house a sizeable collection of antique toys and dolls, while in the south wing there are several interesting displays illustrating Border country life. The informal grounds, with their riverside setting and views of nearby grouse moors, include a woodland walk and picnic tables.

Open Apr–Aug, certain days.

The ancient royal burgh of Linlithgow, now a residential centre, was once one of Scotland's four main towns and an important industrial centre with a reputation that the place was 'smelt before it was seen'. Local industries included mining, textiles, milling, brewing and the manufacture of candles, soap and glue.

Linlithgow Palace is the chief attraction, a well-preserved 15th-century ruin on the side of Linlithgow Loch and the birthplace of Mary Stuart in 1542. The town retains its medieval layout and many fine buildings; these include early 17th-century houses such as Hamilton House, a laird's house of 1628. The 17th-century mercat cross is the only complete cross of its type in the country.

Once this was one of the most important fortresses in Scotland. Used as a state prison during Covenanting times and in the late 19th century as a powder magazine, it was one of four castles left fortified by the Articles of Union. Most impressive are the massive 17th-century artillery emplacements.

Open all year, most days. Closed 25–26 Dec & 1–3 Jan.

An example of changing architectural tastes from 1612 onwards, the House of The Binns reflects the transition from fortified stronghold to spacious mansion. Recent major structural restoration works have now been completed at this fascinating house. It was once a tall, grey, three-storeyed building with small windows and twin turrets; and after additions, reshaping and refacing, it has evolved into a pretty U-shaped house, with crenellations and embellished windows. The most outstanding features are the beautiful early 17th-century moulded plaster ceilings inside. This is the historic home of the Dalyell family, who have lived here since 1612. One of its most colourful characters was General Tam Dalyell, an ardent Royalist who was captured by Cromwell's army at the Battle of Worcester but escaped from the Tower of London and fled to Russia, where he organised the Tsar's army. He

Thirlestane Castle
TEL: 01578 722430

LINLITHGOW
TOWN ON A803, 16 MILES (25.5KM) W OF EDINBURGH

Blackness Castle
(4 MILES N)
TEL: 0131 668 8800

House of The Binns
(4 MILES E OFF A904)
TEL: 01506 834255

was recalled at the Restoration to command Charles II's forces in Scotland, and was the founder of the Royal Scots Greys here in 1681. His boots and comb can still be seen in the house, together with a thimble belonging to his grand-daughter, Magdalen, and the drawings of Sir John Graham Dalyell, who taught Darwin. There are panoramic views over the Firth of Forth from a site in the grounds.

Open: House, May–Sep, most days. Parkland, all year.

Linlithgow Palace
TEL: 0131 668 8800

Rising dramatically from the shores of Linlithgow Loch is a great square palace-fortress, which dates from the 15th century. Although there was a fortified residence here as early as the mid 12th century, and Edward I built a manor here in 1302, it was not until 1425 that work began on the castle that may be seen today.

The Scottish King, James I, gave orders that the royal residence should be constructed on the site of the earlier buildings, and although Linlithgow was primarily a palace, the architect incorporated a number of defensive features. There was a drawbridge and a barbican, and the walls of the four corner towers were immensely thick. The windows in the lower floors were protected by iron bars, the holes for which can still be seen in the stone. Around the early 1500s, machicolations were added. Various rooms remain, including the great hall, with a huge ornate fireplace. There is an octagonal Gothic/Renaissance fountain in the inner courtyard.

One of Scotland's four royal palaces, Linlithgow was built for James I of Scotland

Next door is St Michael's Church, a 13th-century foundation rebuilt after a fire in 1424 and one of Scotland's largest pre-Reformation churches, topped with an aluminium tower added in the 1960s. The nave and choir are a fine composition, and in place of transepts there are two chapels, in the southerly of which James IV had the vision of his coming end at Flanders.

Linlithgow has played its part in Scotland's history. Mary, Queen of Scots was born here in 1542, Charles I slept here in 1633 and Cromwell stayed in the Palace in the winter of 1650–51. When the Duke of Cumberland's army bivouacked in Linlithgow in 1746 en route to their encounter with Price Charles Edward Stuart's army at Culloden Moor, fires were left burning which gutted this handsome building.

Open all year, daily. Closed 25–26 Dec & 1–3 Jan.

A successful New Town, noted for manufacturing and high technology industries, Livingston was established in 1962 in a previous coal-mining and shale oil-extracting area. Adjacent Mid Calder was formerly a coaching stop on the main route from Glasgow to Edinburgh; there is a 16th-century church and connections with John Knox at Calder House. Near by is Almondell and Calderwood Country Park, with its Visitor Centre.

Situated along the banks of the River Almond, the park has been left as

naturally as possible to encourage wildlife. There are paths through woodland and along the riverside. The park's ranger service organises various guided walks and activities such as batwatching, hedge-making and a children's nature club. An aquarium in the Visitor Centre shows different types of water life from river, pond and canal.

A remote village on the southern edge of the Lammermuir Hills. Excellent moorland walking is near by and there is access to the Southern Upland Way.

A village inland from the Firth of Forth, near which stands Gosford House, an 18th-century mansion designed partly by Robert Adam and the seat of the Earls of Wemyss.

LIVINGSTON
New Town off M8, 13 miles (21km) W of Edinburgh

Almondell and Calderwood Country Park
Tel: 01506 882254

LONGFORMACUS
Village off A6105, 6 miles (9.5km) W of Duns

LONGNIDDRY
Village on A198, 3 miles (5km) SW of Aberlady

MELROSE
*TOWN ON A6091, 4 MILES
(6.5KM) E OF GALASHIELS*

Abbotsford House
*(2 MILES/3KM W OFF A6091)
TEL: 01896 752043*

*Abbotsford stands on the
site of the last of the clan
battles in the Borders, a fact
which is wholly in keeping
with Sir Walter Scott's
romantic view of historical
events and which may even
have influenced his choice
of new home.*

Beautifully situated between the River Tweed and the Eildon Hills, Melrose was an important Roman centre. Today, its chief attraction is the stone remains of Melrose Abbey, founded by David I in 1136 to replace the 7th-century monastery of St Aidan, to the east. There is easy access up the Eildon Hills from the town. Abbotsford, the final home of Sir Walter Scott, lies near by on the River Tweed and clearly shows the hand of the writer in its architecture.

Abbotsford is fascinating on two counts – first because it was the home of Sir Walter Scott, and second because of the diverse collections with which the writer filled his house. Many of these collections were brought with him from his former home, just a few miles away at Ashiestiel, and it is said to have been a curious procession which moved up the valley to Abbotsford on 28 May 1812. By this time Sir Walter was already a published writer, with the profits from *The Lay of the Last Minstrel, Marmion* and *The Lady of the Lake* contributing to the purchase of his new home. Two years after moving in he began his Waverley series of novels, and as his success as a writer grew, so too did Abbotsford and its estate.

In 1818 the former farmhouse was extended by the addition of an armoury, a dining room, a study, a conservatory and three extra bedrooms. Then in 1822 the original building was demolished to make way for what is now the main block of Abbotsford. By this time Sir Walter's holdings of land had increased to some 1,400 acres (567ha), which he liberally planted with trees. He died here in 1832. The house was further extended in the 1850s by Sir Walter's descendant, Walter Lockhart Scott, who added a west wing containing the chapel and kitchen, thus completing the attractive composition we see today.

Successive generations of Scotts have made Abbotsford their home, but it remains a splendid memorial to their famous ancestor and all around the house are reminders of him. The study is particularly evocative, with a bronze cast of his head still watching over his writing desk, and shelves and shelves of books which have spilled over from the library. Altogether there are about 9,000 volumes collected by Sir Walter. He looks out over the drawing room, too, from the famous portrait by Raeburn over the fireplace. This is a delightful room, with the Chinese hand-painted wallpaper given to Sir Walter by his cousin, and a roll-top desk and chairs given to him by George IV.

Sir Walter had a fascination for historic weaponry, and his armoury contains an interesting mixture ranging from his own blunderbuss to Rob Roy's broadsword, dirk and sporran purse. Bonnie Dundee's pistol

is here, and the double-barrelled carbine of a Tyrolean patriot.

Other curiosities are dotted around the house, including various relics from the Battle of Waterloo, two cannon balls from the siege of Roxburgh Castle in 1460, a model of the skull of Robert the Bruce and a 'scold's bridle', used to silence nagging wives.

Open late Mar–Oct, daily.

Sit Walter Scott's lovely mansion on the River Tweed is a reminder of a great man

The ruin of this Cistercian abbey is probably one of Scotland's finest, and has been given added glamour by its connection with Sir Walter Scott. The abbey was repeatedly wrecked during the Scottish wars of independence, but parts of the nave and choir survive from the 14th century, and include some of the best and most elaborate traceried stonework in Scotland, and well-preserved Perpendicular windows. Most of the ruins belong to a 15th-century reconstruction. The abbey has many interesting features: the heart of Robert the Bruce is buried somewhere within the church; note too the figure of a pig playing the bagpipes, set on the roof. The museum, sited at the entrance to the ruins and housed in the 16th-century Commendator's House, is an interesting addition to this historic ruin.

Open all year, daily.

Melrose Abbey & Abbey Museum
TEL: 0131 668 8800

Left, the well-preserved ruins of Melrose Abbey

The Priorwood Garden specialises in flowers which are suitable for drying. It is formally designed with herbaceous and everlasting annual borders, and the attractive orchard has a display of 'apples through the ages' including ancient varieties.

Open all year, daily.

Priorwood Garden & Dried Flower Shop
(OFF A6091)
TEL: 01896 822493

This small village north-east of Hawick has the imposing Minto Crags near by. On their summit are the wonderfully named ruins of Fatlips Castle.

MINTO
VILLAGE OFF A698, 5 MILES (8KM) NE OF HAWICK

The village of Morebattle in the northern foothills of the Cheviots is almost encircled by the winding Kale Water. Across the river, to the north of the village, is Linton Church with its fine Norman font. To the south-west lie the massive remnants of the ruined Cressford Castle, with walls 14ft (4m) thick. The castle surrendered to the English in 1545.

MOREBATTLE
VILLAGE ON B6401, 6 MILES (9.5KM) SE OF KELSO

A spacious and attractive old town on the Firth of Forth, known as The Honest Toun. This was a fishing and trading port until the early 19th century, when the harbour silted up. The tollbooth dates from 1591, Pinkie House (now part of a boys' public school) from the 16th century. The golf course was founded in 1774, one of Scotland's oldest. The racecourse first opened in 1816.

(See also Cycle ride: A Circuit East of Edinburgh, page 32.)

MUSSELBURGH
TOWN OFF A1, 6 MILES (9.5KM) E OF EDINBURGH

This planned symmetrical village was founded in 1793 by the Duke of Buccleuch as a handloom weaving centre. Newcastleton is a good base for exploring Liddesdale and the surrounding countryside, being situated on the Liddel Water, which forms the boundary between England and Scotland for some miles.

NEWCASTLETON
VILLAGE ON B6357, 17 MILES (27KM) S OF HAWICK

NEWTONGRANGE
Town on A7, 2 miles (3km) S of Dalkeith

A town in a former coal-mining area. The terraced houses for the miners were laid out in a uniform grid pattern.

Scottish Mining Museum
Lady Victoria Colliery
Tel: 0131 663 7519

Based at the historic Lady Victoria colliery, one of Europe's finest 19th-century collieries, Scotland's National Coal Mining Museum offers entertaining tours led by ex-miners. Visit the pit-head, Scotland's largest steam winding engine, and a full-scale replica of a modern underground coalface. Underground working conditions and life in the mining community are vividly portrayed by an audio-visual show and an award-winning series of life-sized 'talking tableaux'. There is a Visitor Centre with a gift shop and tearoom.

Open Mar–Oct, daily.

NORTH BERWICK
Town on A198, 19 miles (30.5km) E of Edinburgh

A seaside town, once a fishing and trading port and now a popular holiday resort, with a sandy beach, North Berwick was founded earlier than the 12th century. Remains of a 12th-century Cistercian nunnery and a 12th-century parish church are in evidence. North Berwick Museum tells the local story. North Berwick Law, to the south, is a volcanic rock 613ft (184m) high, surmounted by an archway made from a whale's jawbones. To the east, on the coast beyond Canty Bay, are the considerable remains of the picturesque, moated Tantallon Castle.

North Berwick Museum
School Rd
Tel: 01620 895457

The former Burgh School contains a museum with sections on natural history, local history, golf, archaeology and domestic life. Exhibitions are held throughout the summer.

Open Apr–Sep, daily.

Tantallon Castle
(3 miles/5km E on A198)
Tel: 0131 668 8800

The great red walls of Tantallon Castle form one of the strongest and most daunting castles in Scotland. Perched on a spur of rock, with sheer cliffs plummeting into frothing seas on three of its four sides, the fourth side is protected by a formidable array of ditches and walls. Rising from one of the three great gaping ditches, and sweeping clear across the neck of the promontory, is a vast curtain of red sandstone. This wall is 12 feet (3.7m) thick, and a staggering 50 feet (15m) tall. Although cannons and storms have battered this mighty wall, it remains one of the most impressive defensive features of any castle in Britain.

Tantallon is associated with one of Scotland's most famous families – the Red Douglases, Earls of Angus. It came into their hands at the end of the 14th century, and became their base as they plotted and fought against their enemies. But it was not until 1528 that the mighty fortress of Tantallon was seriously put to the test, when King James V himself laid siege to the Red Douglas stronghold.

Sixteenth-century Scottish politics were complicated, but, essentially, Archibald Douglas, 6th Earl of Angus, had kept the young James V a virtual prisoner in Edinburgh during his minority. James finally managed to escape, and once he was old enough to act for himself, he charged Douglas with treason. James brought a great battery of guns from Dunbar Castle, and for 20 days pounded the walls of Tantallon with everything he had. Tantallon, however, stood firm – perhaps because the great ditches to the front of the castle prevented the guns from being brought too close, and perhaps because the king ran short of powder and shot. The castle eventually fell to James, but as a result of negotiations rather than firepower. Douglas fled the country, and James began work to reinforce and repair Tantallon's medieval defences. After the king's death, Douglas returned from exile in 1543 and immediately began plotting against the Regent of Scotland, the Earl of Arran.

The ruins of Tantallon are impressive and the Mid Tower, which has been changed and developed through the centuries, stands almost complete. It was originally five storeys, but suffered during the 1528 siege. In 1556, a Fore Tower was added, designed both to withstand and to house cannon. The East Tower was also five storeys, and there are still stairs in the massive curtain wall that lead to the battlements.

Open all year, most days. Closed 25–26 Dec & 1–3 Jan.

Tantallon, with its towering red sandstone walls poised on the edge of the cliffs, is a spectacular sight

OLDHAMSTOCKS
VILLAGE OFF A1, 6 MILES
(9.5KM) SE OF DUNBAR

This upland village is set about a spacious green. Its name comes from the Saxon for 'old settlement'. A tower in the churchyard was built to watch over graves and prevent body-snatching.

ORMISTON
VILLAGE ON B6371, 2 MILES
(3KM) S OF TRANENT

This planned village (1735) on the Tyne Water has a wide green and an attractive layout. There is a simple yet important 15th-century mercat cross.

PEEBLES
TOWN ON A703, 20 MILES
(32KM) S OF EDINBURGH

This attractive old royal burgh on the River Tweed is popular as a holiday town and woollen-manufacturing centre. The Beltane Festival in June includes a Common Riding of the Marches. To the west lies 14th-century Neidpath Castle, a tower house with pit prison. To the east are Kailzie Gardens. Peebles is also a good angling centre. To the east of the town, and bordering the Innerleithen road, lies Glentress Forest.
(See also Picnic: Glentress Forest, page 46.)

Kailzie Gardens
(2½ MILES/4KM SE
ON B7062)
TEL: 01721 720007

These extensive grounds with their fine old trees provide a burnside walk flanked by bulbs, rhododendrons and azaleas. A walled garden contains herbaceous, shrub rose borders, greenhouses and a small formal rose garden. There is a waterfowl pond, an art gallery, and a childrens' play area.
Open late Mar–Oct, daily. Grounds close 5.30pm. Garden open all year.

Neidpath Castle
(1 MILE/1.5KM W ON A72)
TEL: 01721 720333

After Scotland had won her independence from England in the 14th century under great warriors like William Wallace and Robert the Bruce, local landowners had the task of establishing law and order in their domains. Castles such as the one at Neidpath were built, not only to provide a form of defence should the laird come under attack, but also so that he could maintain a tighter control over his subjects.
Neidpath's L-plan tower was built in the second half of the 14th century, and the upper two floors were remodelled in the 17th century. The tower is unusual, because both arms of the L form parallelograms, rather than rectangles as was most common, and the corners are rounded. It is an intriguing building, its four main floors intersected with mural passages and 'entresols', or mezzanine floors, giving the impression that the castle is full of small chambers and passages, all at different heights.
The lower floor contained a pit prison and a well, while on the second floor is a room with some fine 17th-century panelling. Mary, Queen of Scots and James I and VI are both known to have stayed at Neidpath, although the castle has been too much altered since the 16th century to be able to identify which rooms they occupied.

Gazetteer

It was, however, successively owned by the families of Fraser, Hay (Earl of Tweeddale), Douglas (Earl of March) and Wemyss (Earl of Wemyss and March).

There are picturesque views, fine walls and a picnic area.

Open early Apr–Sep, daily.

This planned village of 1770 is now a sizeable town. It was a paper-making and cotton industry centre, and is now home to the Edinburgh Crystal Glass Works. The belfry of the parish church dates from the 12th century. During the Napoleonic wars, Valleyfield Mill was used to confine French prisoners, 300 of whom died there and are commemorated by a monument.

A tour around the factory allows visitors to see the various stages in the art of glassmaking, including glass blowing, the 'lehr', cutting, polishing, engraving and sand etching. An exhibition and video entitled The Story of Edinburgh Crystal explains the process further.

Open all year. Tours most days. Closed 25–27 Dec & 1–2 Jan.

This hill lies north of Jedburgh, and is topped by a well-known Border landmark, the Waterloo Monument, erected in 1815 by the Marquis of Lothian.

The massive tower and turrets of Neidpath Castle rise dramatically from the rock above the River Tweed

PENICUIK
TOWN ON A701, 19 MILES (30.5KM) S OF EDINBURGH

Edinburgh Crystal Visitor Centre
EASTFIELD INDUSTRIAL ESTATE
TEL: 01968 675128

PENIEL HEUGH
HILL OFF B6400, 4 MILES (6.5KM) N OF JEDBURGH

*A*n exhilarating hill walk only a few miles from Edinburgh, between two picturesque reservoirs in the Pentland Hills. The walk affords spectacular views, as well as the chance to see a variety of plants and birds.

Grid ref: NT233631

INFORMATION

The walk is 9 miles (14.5km) long and climbs about 450ft.
Stout footwear is essential.
Dogs should be kept on a lead.
The Flotterstone Inn serves food.

Picnic/barbecue site, children's play area at Visitor Centre.
Toilets at Visitor Centre.

START

Park at the Flotterstone Visitor Centre. This is just off the A702,

south of Edinburgh; turn right at the Flotterstone Inn and drive past the inn for about 100yds (91.5m) to the Visitor Centre and car park.

DIRECTIONS

From the Visitor Centre take the path through the woods, which runs parallel with and eventually joins the road. Carry on along the road, passing the firing range to your right and a wood and Glen Cottage to your left. About ½ mile (1km) after Glen Cottage the road curves left and crosses a stone bridge. Shortly after this bridge turn right through a gate

Glencorse Reservoir

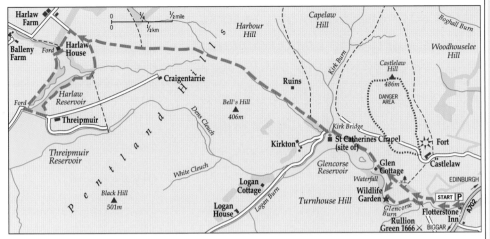

(signposted 'Balerno, Currie and Colinton').

Follow this path up the hill. At the fork bear left (signposted to Currie and Balerno) and continue along this path, passing a ruined cottage to your right. When you reach the wall, cross using the stone stile and follow the path as it curves left and proceeds downhill to reach a gate.

Cross the stile and go straight on (for 'Balerno'). Cross another stile and proceed along the edge of a field. Follow the path as it curves left and shortly meets another path. Turn right onto this path. Just before the metal gate turn left onto a tarmac road. Follow the road as it curves left, towards a house. Immediately past the house turn right.

Cross the ford using the metal footbridge, and carry on along the path. Cross another ford and turn left, and follow the path through the wood, with the wall to your right. After about 200yds

(183m) turn left and continue along the path around the edge of Threipmuir Reservoir. When eventually you reach a wooden stile, cross the wall. Turn left, cross another stile and continue along the track, with a fence to your left. At a wooden post on your left turn right.

Retrace your steps to Glen Cottage. Shortly beyond Glen Cottage, at the edge of the wood, turn right. Follow this path down through the wood and round a left curve. On your right you will see a Wildlife Garden and tree nursery. Carry on along

the path until it rejoins the road and retrace your steps to the car park.

Glencorse Reservoir
The reservoir, built in 1822, contains the submerged remains of St Catherine's Chapel, a 13th-century chapel built by Sir William St Clair of Roslin.

The path through Maiden's Cleuch was an old drove road leading from Balerno and Currie to a sheep market at House o' Muir, just south of Flotterstone. (See also Walk: Pentlands Reservoir, page 74.)

WHAT TO LOOK OUT FOR

Birds that may be seen include red grouse, curlew, skylark and golden plover, and waterfowl such as goosander, tufted duck and geese.
Look out for the spectacular waterfall to your right just before the path curves left towards the Wildlife Garden.

This easy walk below the Pentland Hills, just outside Edinburgh, takes in woodland and an attractive reservoir with plenty of birdlife. The walk starts and finishes at a Visitor Centre with wildlife displays and a children's play area.

Grid ref: NT233631
INFORMATION

The walk is about 3 miles (5km) long.

Easy going on good paths or tracks.

Some road walking.

Dogs should be kept on leads.

The Flotterstone Inn, open all day, serves bar meals; children welcome.

Toilets at Visitor Centre.

START

Flotterstone is on the A702, south of Edinburgh, easily reached from the city or the ring road. Drive past the inn for about 100yds (91.5m) to reach the Visitor Centre car park.

DIRECTIONS

From the Visitor Centre, follow the path that runs parallel to the road, then join the road and continue straight on. On the right is a military training area. Reach Glencorse Reservoir and continue along the road beside the water returning the same way. (You can, of course, continue along the road as far as you wish before turning back.) On the return, just before the end of the wood,

where there are some fine old pines, turn right through a gate and walk down a track beside a burn. On the right is a wildlife garden and tree nursery. Continue along the track, through two gates, and eventually rejoin the road and path back to the Centre.

Glencorse Reservoir

Glencorse is known as the 'Queen of the Pentland Reservoirs' – there are 11 such stretches of water around the hills, providing for the need of thirsty Edinburgh. The reservoir was built in 1822 and has a maximum depth of 71 feet (22m); it holds 367 million gallons of water. All this area is now part of the Pentland Hills Regional Park, a large and beautiful stretch of country managed on a co-operative basis by landowners, local authorities and voluntary bodies for conservation, recreation and agriculture.

(See also page 72.)

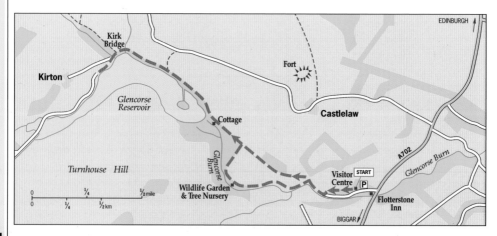

Wildlife Garden and Tree Nursery

Down by the burn on the return walk is an interesting small wildlife garden and a tree nursery, cultivating many different species, which helps to replenish stocks in the woodland.

You will also find here a small enclosure called 'Forever Green'.

WHAT TO LOOK OUT FOR

You should see a variety of waterfowl on the reservoir, especially in winter – look for tufted duck, pochard, goosander and wigeon.
You may also see squirrels as well as birds in the woods.

The pochard is one of the most familiar diving ducks

PRESTONPANS
TOWN ON B1348, 3 MILES (5KM) NE OF MUSSELBURGH

▷ A medieval mining and salt-producing town, once noted for oysters, with a good range of laird's houses of different dates, including the 15th-century Preston Tower and Hamilton House (1628). It has a complete and unaltered 17th-century mercat cross. Prestongrange Industrial Heritage Museum covers 800 years of mining history. This was the site of the Battle of Prestonpans (1745), which resulted in a Jacobite victory over General Cope; a cairn commemorates the battle.

(See also Cycle ride: A Circuit East of Edinburgh, page 32.)

Prestongrange Industrial Heritage Museum
PRESTONGRANGE
TEL: 0131 653 2904

▷ The oldest documented coal mining site in Britain with 800 years of history, this museum shows a Cornish beam engine and on-site evidence of associated industries such as brickmaking and pottery, plus a 16th-century customs port. The 'Cutting the Coal' exhibition, in the David Space Gallery, has an underground gallery, a coalface, a reconstruction of a colliery workshop and a wonderful collection of coal-cutting machines and equipment. There is a guided tour of the site by a former miner.

Open Apr–Sep, daily.

(See also Cycle ride: A Circuit East of Edinburgh, page 32.)

RATHO
VILLAGE OFF B7030, 8 MILES (13KM) W OF EDINBURGH

▷ This village is popular as a canal-boating centre on the Forth-Clyde Canal. Ratho is also the site of an impressive railway viaduct. The restored church dates from the 12th century.

ROMANNO BRIDGE
VILLAGE ON A701, 3 MILES (5KM) S OF WEST LINTON

▷ A small village on the Lyne Water; near by are the 'Romanno Terraces', believed to be the remnants of medieval cultivation platforms cut out of the hillside.

ROSLIN (OR ROSSLYN)
VILLAGE OFF A701, 2 MILES (3KM) S OF LOANHEAD

▷ This mining village lies on the River North Esk, in the vicinity of which was fought a battle in 1303 when the Scots defeated the English invaders. Roslin is famous both for its chapel and its castle. Roslin Castle was built by the St Clair family (of Norman origin) in the 15th century. It stands on a dramatic site high above Roslin Glen, and was restored in the 1580s, with 16th- and 17th-century additions. In the 15th century the St Clair family was wealthy enough to dine from gold and silver tableware. At one time Sir William St Clair was so rich and powerful he could mint his own coins.

The chapel was destined to be an enormous cruciform church, but the building work that commenced in 1446 was never completed. However, there exists magnificently decorated and ornate stonework, which has a theme of flowers and foliage. There are lilies and roses on the roof to symbolise love and peace, and cabbages and kale on pillars, including the famous spiral 'Prentice Pillar', to symbolise

thanksgiving. Many members of the family are buried in the deep vaults, some reputedly still wearing full armour.

St Abb (Ebba or Aebbe) was the daughter of Edifred, King of Northumbria. Legend has it that she went to sea to escape the attention of the King of Mercia, was shipwrecked and washed up hereabouts. In gratitude for her safe delivery (from the shipwreck, that is, not the king), she founded a double monastery-nunnery, and governed it as abbess until she died in AD 683. St Cuthbert visited her in 661. The abbey buildings were destroyed, probably by the Vikings, though there are some remains of a later foundation in her name a mile or so inland. The village lived by its fishing (and its smuggling) for centuries; lobster and crab boats still operate from here, but now it is also a holiday village, with one of the few sandy beaches on this spectacular stretch of cliff-bound coast. It clings to the cliffs, some houses looking down from the top, another group of old fisherman's cottages (now holiday homes) lower down, overlooking the little harbour and lifeboat station. Beside the harbour is a picturesque row of ageing wooden net-huts used for storing fishermen's gear. The whole place is brightly coloured, with the orangey-red of pantiled roofs set off by the mix-and-match colours of the painted stone walls of the terraced houses.

ST ABBS
VILLAGE OFF A1107, 12 MILES (19KM) N OF BERWICK-UPON-TWEED

St Abb's Head, just to the north of the village, is a National Nature Reserve, noted particularly for its nesting seabirds, including guillemots, razorbills, kittiwakes, shags, fulmars and eiders. The walk out there along the cliffs is a spectacular one.

Looking down on to the harbour and the lifeobat station

ST BOSWELLS
VILLAGE ON A68, 4 MILES (6.5KM) SE OF MELROSE

St Boswells boasts Scotland's largest village green, once the venue for horse and cattle fairs. Nearby Mertoun Gardens have shrubs, trees and a walled garden in a beautiful position.

ST MARY'S LOCH
LOCH ON A708, 13 MILES (21KM) W OF SELKIRK

This stretch of water includes Loch of the Lowes. Tibbie Shiels inn on its banks has literary connections: near by is a statue of the poet James Hogg.

SELKIRK
TOWN ON A7, 9 MILES (14.5KM) N OF HAWICK

An ancient tweed-manufacturing royal burgh above the Ettrick and Yarrow valleys. Halliwells House is a museum telling the story of the industrialisation of the Tweed Valley. A statue shows the explorer Mungo Park (1771–1806), who was born locally. Flodden Monument was erected in 1913. About 3 miles (5km) west is Bowhill House, a Georgian mansion with superb French antiques and European paintings.

Bowhill House and Country Park
(3 MILES/5KM W OF SELKIRK, OFF A708)
TEL: 01750 22204

An outstanding collection of pictures, including works by Van Dyck, Canaletto, Reynolds, Gainsborough and Claude Lorraine, are displayed in this, the Border home of the Duke of Buccleuch and Queensberry. In addition to these there is an equally stunning collection of porcelain and furniture, much of it made in the Paris workshop of André Boulle. Memorabilia and relics of people such as Queen Victoria and Sir Walter Scott, and a restored Victorian kitchen add further interest inside the house.

Outside, the wooded grounds are perfect for walking. Children will enjoy the adventure playground and, no doubt, the gift shop. There is also a theatre and an audio-visual display. Art courses are held here.

Open, park: May–Aug, most days; house: Jul, daily.

Halliwells House Museum
HALLIWELLS CLOSE, MARKET PLACE
TEL: 01750 20096

The former role of Selkirk's oldest surviving dwelling has been recreated in this enterprising museum. The home and ironmonger's shop, lovingly restored, can be seen together with the story of the town's development and frequent temporary exhibitions.

Open Apr–Nov, daily.

Sir Walter Scott's Courtroom
MARKET PLACE
TEL: 01750 20096

Built in 1804 as the new sheriff court and town house for Selkirk, it was here that the novelist Sir Walter Scott pursued his work as Sheriff of the County of Selkirk. It is now re-opened as a museum with displays and audio-visual presentations about Scott's life, his writing, his contemporaries (James Hogg and Mungo Park) and his time as sheriff.

Open Apr–Oct, daily.

gazetteer

Preston Palace was replaced in 1790 by Robert Adam's Seton Castle. Seton collegiate church stands in the grounds, unfinished, but with remarkable vaulted apses, a piscina and interesting tombs.

The main feature of this village is the well-preserved Smailholm Tower. The views from here are excellent.

An outstanding example of a classic Border tower-house, probably erected in the 15th century. It is 57ft (17.5m) high and stands on a high outcrop near the village. The tower houses an exhibition of dolls and a display based on Sir Walter Scott's work *Minstrelsy of the Scottish Border*. It consists of tapestries and costume figures.

Originally a pilgrim ferry port, South Queensferry was founded by St Margaret of Scotland in the 11th century; trade was important in the 16th and 17th centuries. Queensferry Museum relates the local history. The former ferry boats left from the Hawes Pier, opposite which stands the Howes inn (1683), described in Sir Walter Scott's *The Antiquary* and Robert Louis Stevenson's *Kidnapped*. Nearby Hopetoun House, designed by William Bruce in 1699–1702, with Adam additions from 1721, epitomises the great country house.

This is the home of the Earl and the Countess of Rosebery, whose family have lived here for over 300 years. The house, however, only dates from 1815 when it was built in Tudor Gothic style. There are vaulted corridors and a splendid Gothic hammerbeamed hall, but the main rooms are in classical style. Dalmeny House has a magnificent situation on the Firth of Forth and there are delightful walks in the wooded grounds and along the shore. Inside, it has fine French furniture, tapestries and porcelain from the Rothschild Mentmore collection. Early Scottish furniture is also shown, with 18th-century portraits, Rosebery racing mementos and a display of pictures associated with Napoleon.

Open Jul–early Sep, certain days.

(See also page 12.)

Situated on a green island on the Firth of Forth, the Augustinian abbey was founded in about 1123 by Alexander I. The well-preserved remains include a 13th-century octagonal chapter house and wall painting. Access to the island is by ferry April to September.

Open Apr–Sep, daily.

SETON MAINS
SITE ON A198, 3 MILES (5KM). E OF PRESTONPANS

SMAILHOLM
VILLAGE ON B6397, 5 MILES (8KM) W OF KELSO

Smailholm Tower
(1.5 MILES/2.5KM SW ON B6937)
TEL: 0131 668 8800

SOUTH QUEENSFERRY
SMALL TOWN OFF A90, AT S END OF FORTH BRIDGES

Dalmeny House
TEL: 0131 331 1888

Inchcolm Abbey
INCHCOLM ISLAND (1½ MILES/2.5KM S OF ABERDOUR
TEL: 0131 668 8800

Queensferry Museum
53 HIGH ST
TEL: 0131 331 5545

The museum tells the story of South Queensferry and its people. It looks at the development of the Queensferry Passage, the growth of the former Royal Burgh and the building of the rail and road bridges which span the Forth. There are displays on the life work and pastimes of Queensferry people and a life-sized model of the Burry Man, part of a centuries-old custom. There are changing exhibitions and a new 'hands-on' display on the natural history of the Forth.

Open all year, most days.

Hopetoun House
*(2 MILES/3KM W OF FORTH
ROAD BRIDGE, OFF B904)*
TEL: 0131 331 2451

When King George IV came to Hopetoun in 1822 the ceremonials were masterminded by Sir Walter Scott. With the 4th Earl of Hopetoun as their Captain-General, a company of gentlemen archers formed a guard of honour for the King's arrival. He was so impressed that the company were granted the title of 'King's Bodyguard in Scotland' – a ceremonial role which continues to this day.

A swathe of grassy parkland cuts through the wooded southern shore of the Firth of Forth and at its centre stands one of Scotland's most splendid mansions, Hopetoun House, the home of the Marquess of Linlithgow. Begun in 1699, it is the creation of two of Scotland's most celebrated architects – Sir William Bruce, who was responsible for the original building, and William Adam, who enlarged it some time later.

The Marquess's ancestors, the Hope family, were diligent in their public service and in their studies of the law and the sciences. In the 17th century Sir Thomas Hope rose to become Charles I's King's Advocate, and his sons followed him into the legal profession. It was his grandson, John Hope, who purchased the land on which Hopetoun House now stands.

Hopetoun's interiors are a sumptuous progression of richly decorated rooms which provide a suitably grand setting for the fine works of art, including notable paintings by such artists as Canaletto, Gainsborough and Raeburn, displayed within them. The red drawing room, with its scarlet damask wall covering and intricate gilded plaster ceiling, is one of the most magnificent rococo rooms in Scotland, while the gold state dining room is a set piece of the Regency period. Hot food would have been brought here from the kitchen in a steam-heated container, pushed along a railway track, then raised in a lift to a warming oven from where it was served by the butler and footmen. This is also where the family portraits are congregated.

The front stairs are an important feature of the original house and are in complete contrast to the state apartments, having mellow pine panelling with painted panels and borders which are beautifully carved with flowers, fruit, corn stalks and peapods.

One unusual attraction at Hopetoun House is the roof-top viewing platform. The wonderful panorama over the surrounding grounds to the countryside beyond and, of course, the Forth, with its famous bridges away to the east, is well worth the climb. The grounds are extensive, and include deer parks with red and fallow deer, and a herd of the rare St Kilda sheep. There are formal gardens as well, and it is possible to play croquet or pétanque for a fee.

Hopetoun also has a number of special exhibitions, including a family museum and 'The Building of Hopetoun', commemorating the architects and craftspeople whose talents combined to create this magnificent building. The contracts and accounts make fascinating reading. Out in the tack room off the courtyard is a display, entitled 'Horse and Man in Lowland Scotland', devoted to the role played by the horse in the economic and social life of the area before the motor vehicle took over.

Open Apr–early Oct, daily.

The rococo elegance of Hopetoun's interior

SOUTRA HILL
HILL OFF B6368, 4 MILES (6.5KM) N OF OXTON

A noted viewpoint on the road between Moorfoot and the Lammermuir Hills, south-east of Edinburgh. Soutra Aisle is a remnant of a 15th-century hospice.

STENTON
VILLAGE ON B6370, 5 MILES (8KM) SE OF DUNBAR

A pretty village with a medieval wool stone on the green and a 14th-century rood well. The 16th-century Biel terraced gardens lie to the north-east.

STOBO
VILLAGE ON B712, 8 MILES (13KM) SW OF PEEBLES

The small restored church of Stobo, overlooking the River Tweed, is of Norman date, with 16th- and 17th-century additions. The barrel-vaulted porch enshrines a 13th-century doorway, and the ancient jougs, or iron collar for wrongdoers, still hang by the porch. Dawyck Botanic Garden is where the horse-chestnut was introduced to Scotland in 1650 and the larch in 1725.

Dawyck Botanic Garden
TEL: 01721 760254

An impressive collection of mature specimen trees, some over 131ft (40m) tall, provide an imposing setting for a variety of flowering trees, shrubs and herbaceous plants. Landscaped walks lead visitors through mature woodland which is full of wildlife.
   Open mid Mar–late Oct, daily.

TORPICHEN
VILLAGE ON B792, 2 MILES (3KM) N OF BATHGATE

This pretty hill-backed village was founded as the only Scottish house of the Knights of St John of Jerusalem, and was an important medieval sanctuary. Part of the original church was incorporated into the present 17th-century parish church, a fine example of fortified church architecture. Torpichen Mill was the birthplace, in 1767, of Henry Bell, designer of one of the earliest steamboats, the *Comet*. The top of nearby Cairnpapple Hill is the site of an underground burial cist used for ritual from about 2500 BC.

TRANENT
TOWN OFF A1, 4 MILES (6.5KM) E OF MUSSELBURGH

This industrial and mining town lies a little inland from the Firth of Forth. The church dates from 1800 with a 1587 dovecote near by.

TRAPRAIN LAW
HILL OFF A1, 2 MILES (3KM) SW OF EAST LOTHIAN

A distinctively shaped hill 734ft (220m) and well-known landmark formed by volcanic activity. The summit was the site of a late Bronze Age settlement protected by turf ramparts. In about 700 BC more substantial stone ramparts were built. Later it became the capital of the Votadini tribe which ruled much of the Lothians and Borders around the time of the Roman occupation. Excavations in 1919 uncovered a remarkable collection of Roman silver including jugs, bowls, goblets and spoons, dating from about AD 415. The silver is now in the National Museum of Antiquities, Edinburgh.

Walk

*T*his walk takes you through the pleasantly rolling East Lothian countryside and touches on various aspects of the history of the area over the last 3,000 years.

Grid ref: NT592772
INFORMATION
The walk is about 6 miles (9.5km) long.
Walking includes narrow tracks which can be soft and muddy. Some road walking on quiet lanes – children and dogs should be under control.
The climb to the summit of Traprain Law is steep but worth the effort.
Cafés and pubs in East Linton.

START
East Linton is 25 miles (40km) east of Edinburgh. Turn off the A1 into East Linton; just after passing under the railway bridge, turn left again into the village. There is ample parking in the village centre.

DIRECTIONS
From the village centre retrace your steps but instead of turning right under the railway bridge, turn left past the Red Lion Hotel, to cross the River Tyne on the 16th-century bridge which once carried the great mail road between Edinburgh and London. Turn right at Lauder Place to pass under the railway, and go up to

the A1. The A1 can be very busy, so cross over with great care, and follow signs to Hailes Castle along the quiet, narrow road known as Brae Heads Loan. This road passes high above the River Tyne which flows through a deep valley below and gives excellent views west over the rolling countryside.

Just before reaching Hailes Castle, opposite the lay-by marked as parking for visitors to the castle, turn left up the lane. This is a well worn but rough track barred in places by gates which can be climbed or circumnavigated. The track winds its way between arable fields and rough ground eventually joining a

minor road. Turn left onto this road; carry on past the first gate and stile on to the Law, to another gate and stile 200yds (183m) on, where there are some information boards – well worth reading before you start your ascent. The zig-zag path to the summit is waymarked but leaves a lot to common sense. At the top take time to catch your breath and enjoy the views. Retrace your steps down the hill, and take the same track back to Hailes Castle. This walk in the opposite direction offers a whole new range of views to East Linton and beyond.

Hailes Castle, once a medieval stronghold

HAILES CASTLE AND TRAPRAIN LAW

Pass Hailes Castle on the left and head back along Brae Heads Loan for about 50yds (46m). Take the narrow path left, leading down towards the river, and cross via the wooden foot bridge.

Follow the rough path along the north bank of the river. The path is clearly defined: there is one stile and a series of wooden steps to overcome where the river passes through a steep, rocky gorge.

The path continues under the A1 and passes by the edge of a garden before arriving back at East Linton.

WHAT TO LOOK OUT FOR

Although this area is heavily farmed there are still hedges and small copses and patches of rough ground where a wide variety of wildlife can be found. The slopes of Traprain Law are particularly rich in plant life, and in spring the banks of the Tyne are carpeted in snowdrops, to be followed by wild daffodils.

Hailes Castle

This 13th- to 14th-century castle was built by the Earls of Dunbar, and then became a stronghold of the Gourlay family before passing to the Hepburns. James Hepburn,

The view from the castle

the Earl of Bothwell, brought Mary, Queen of Scots here in 1567. The castle was partially destroyed in 1650 by Cromwell's troops.

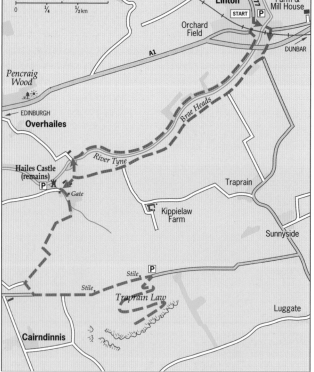

An attractive village with Scotland's oldest inhabited house at its centre. Traquair means 'the village on the winding stream'.

Traquair is the oldest inhabited house in Scotland, and it is also among the most romantic. It was built in the 10th century and has been visited by no fewer than 27 monarchs over the years – William the Lion held court here, and there are particularly strong links with Mary, Queen of Scots and with the Jacobite cause. During the Civil War the then Earl could not quite decide which side to support, and so took no active part himself, but he sent his son to join his kinsman Montrose before the battle of Philiphaugh. Shortly afterwards, however, when the fleeing Montrose sought refuge at Traquair, the Earl pretended he was not at home.

TRAQUAIR
VILLAGE ON B709, 1 MILE (1.5KM) S OF INNERLEITHEN

Traquair House
TEL: 01896 830323 & 830785

The large Bear Gates, once the main entrance to Traquair, were closed in 1745, not to be re-opened until there was once again a Stuart on the throne. Ever since that day a new drive to the house, running parallel to the old avenue, has been used.

The mellow old house of Traquair began its existence as a royal hunting lodge

'The wind through the rusted
  iron sings,
The sun on the self-sown
  tangle burns,
But never a hoof on the
  roadway rings –
The gate is shut till the King
  returns.'
W H Ogilvie

The Library, Traquair House

The house reflects every moment of its 800 years of history, with ancient stone walls, a 'modern' wing, dating from 1680, and furniture and contents which span many centuries. The Museum Room is particularly absorbing, with items ranging from Mary, Queen of Scots' rosary and crucifix to a 16th-century calculator and a lengthy list (in her own hand) of the 4th Countess's children.

Traquair remains at the heart of a working estate which includes Britain's oldest surviving (18th-century) working brewery, revived to full working order in 1965. This is licensed to make and sell its own beer.

Outside, there is a maze, croquet, and the opportunity for woodland walks by the River Tweed. There are also craft workshops and an art gallery.

Open early Apr–Sep daily; Oct, certain days. Grounds open Apr–Sep.

*T*his is a lovely short walk through the woodlands within the grounds of Scotland's oldest inhabited house. There is also a delightful old tearoom. The walk is only accessible from April to September.

Grid ref: NT331354

INFORMATION

The walk is 1 mile (1.5km) long; 1½ miles (2.5km) if you include the maze.

Easy ground.

No road walking.

One stile.

Cottage tearoom at Traquair House.

Picnic area near the car park.

Toilet facilities at Traquair House.

START

Traquair House is off the B709, 6 miles (9.5km) south-east of Peebles. Start the walk just outside the courtyard gates by the garden. There is a car park next to the 'wineglass lawn' (entry charge for house and grounds).

 WHAT TO LOOK OUT FOR

Look out for the famous Bear Gates at the end of a long tree-lined avenue, near the entrance. They were closed in 1745 after the Jacobite Rebellion, when the fifth Earl of Traquair promised that they would remain shut until the Stuarts regained the throne. Traquair has extensive ancient woodland. There are stately beeches which allow nothing to grow under their canopies, old oaks which support more species of insect than any other trees, and numerous ancient firs and yew trees. A row of poplars next to the maze is particularly striking. In winter bramblings and chaffinches feed on the woodland floor, especially under the beeches. Grey herons and kingfishers may be seen along the banks of the Tweed.

DIRECTIONS

Come out of the courtyard and turn left. Proceed through a stone doorway straight ahead, past garden and beech hedge and a croquet lawn on your left. Turn left after the wickerwork summerhouse and two huge horse chestnut trees. When you reach the Quair Burn, veer left through some lovely old yew trees and massive firs. Continue left along the bank of the river. Go through a swing gate and bear left diagonally across the meadow until you come to a stile (across the meadow on your right you can see where Quair Burn flows into the River Tweed). Cross the stile and turn right. Walk up the side of the fence with the River Tweed on your right. After about 50yds (45m) turn left into woodland. Follow the path through woodland, and across three footbridges. After crossing the third footbridge turn left. On reaching the drive by the house turn right, passing the brewery on your left and the Well Pool on your right. At the junction turn left, back towards the car park.

Traquair House

Romantic Traquair House, dating from the 10th century, is steeped in history. This is where Alexander I signed a charter, and William the Lion held court here in 1209. Many kings and nobles used to visit the estate for fishing, hunting and hawking. The house has a splendid library and a fine collection of tapestries, family relics, antiques and paintings. There is a restaurant, a tearoom, gift shop, art gallery and craft workshops.

Traquair's 18th-century brewery produces up to 60,000 bottles of beer each year and is open to visitors.

(See also page 85.)

Below and right, the house and grounds

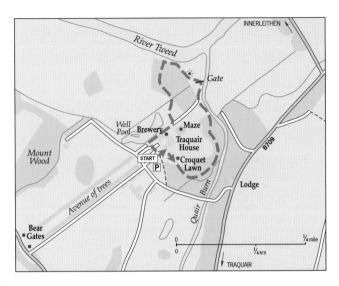

This village at the foot of Talla Reservoir was built in 1905 to provide Edinburgh's water. Near the church is a standing stone 5ft (1.5m) high; in the churchyard is an inscribed Covenanter's Stone dated 1685. The writer John Buchan spent part of his youth in this parish at the south-western extremity of Tweeddale, and his novels include much local colour.

TWEEDSMUIR
VILLAGE ON A701, 8 MILES (13KM) S OF BROUGHTON

This attractive estate village was built in the 17th century to serve Tyninghame House, which was transformed in the 1820s into a Scottish baronial mansion. Beyond the park stretch the Links, terminating in a narrow promontory with a rock known as St Baldred's Castle. Near by is a cairn dating from the Bronze Age. Further north are the Peffer Sands.

TYNINGHAME
VILLAGE ON B1407, 2 MILES (3KM) NE OF EAST LINTON

A village on the River Tweed founded in 1854 for textile-manufacturing. On Purvis Hill, to the north and high above the Tweed, are some remarkable earthen terraces. To the east, and on the south bank of the river is the ruined 16th-century Elibank Tower.

WALKERBURN
VILLAGE ON A72, 2 MILES (3KM) E OF INNERLEITHEN

The river flows from the Pentland Hills south-west of Edinburgh, north-east through Balerno and Edinburgh to the Firth of Forth at Leith, dropping over 1,250ft (381m) in 20 miles (32km). It was formerly used as a power-source for mills, particularly at Dean Village, now a conservation area of Edinburgh with attractive old buildings. A pleasant 13-mile (21-km) walkway runs beside the Water into Edinburgh.

WATER OF LEITH
RIVER

The Tweed Valley south of Walkerburn

West Linton's main street

WEST LINTON
VILLAGE ON A702, 7 MILES (11KM) SW OF PENICUIK

A picturesque village on the edge of the Pentland Hills, which was once an important toll point on the north-west drove road, and noted for its large sheep fairs. The Whipman Society formed in 1803, a horseman's mutual aid society, still holds an annual week of celebration in June. West Linton is noted for its stone-carving, with fine examples in the main street and old churchyard.

WHITEKIRK
VILLAGE ON A198, 4 MILES (6.5KM) SE OF NORTH BERWICK

Whitekirk was once renowned for its healing well, which was visited, among others, by Aeneas Silrius, later Pope Pius II. There is an interesting 15th-century cruciform church with a barrel-vaulted chancel and porch and a massive tower. Near the church is a two-storeyed tithe barn, with part of a 16th-century castle. It was once used for the storage of grain by monks from Holyrood.

LISTINGS

ACTIVITIES

ANGLING

There are many excellent opportunities for salmon and trout fishing, and also sea-angling in this part of Scotland. Salmon fishing need not be expensive, as there are many low-cost stretches of river, managed by local angling associations. Plenty of these will issue permits to non-members.

General enquiries concerning fishing on the River Tweed and tributaries are dealt with by the Tweed Foundation, tel: 01896 848271.

GOLF

This area is wall-to-wall with courses and seaside links of incredible calibre. There are historic, Victorian courses which were created during the boom of 100 years ago, and there are modern courses. Here follows a list of some of the best courses in this area.

Edinburgh courses

Baberton
50 Baberton Av, Juniper Green.
Tel: 0131 453 4911
Parkland course. 18 holes, 6,123yds, Par 69.
Visitors: may not play at weekends or after 3.30pm weekdays. Contact in advance.

Braid Hills
Braid Hills Approach.
Tel: 0131 447 6666
Municipal heathland course with good views of Edinburgh and the Firth of Forth. Course No 1: 18 holes, 6,172yds, Par 70. Course No 2: 18

holes, 4,832yds, Par 65.
Visitors: may not play on Sat mornings.
Bruntsfield Links Golfing Society
32 Barnton Av. Tel: 0131 336 1479
Parkland course with good views of Forth Estuary. 18 holes, 6,407yds, Par 71.
Visitors: must contact in advance.

Carrick Knowe
Carrick Knowe Municipal, Glendevon Park. Tel: 0131 337 1096
Flat parkland course. Played over by 2 clubs, Carrick Knowe and Carrick Vale. 18 holes, 6,299yds, Par 71.
Visitors: may be restricted at weekends.

Craigentinny
Fillyside Rd, Lochend.
Tel: 0131 554 7501
To the north east of Edinburgh, between Leith and Portobello. It is generally flat although there are some hillocks with gentle slopes. The famous Arthur's Seat dominates the southern skyline. 18 holes, 5,418yds, Par 67.
Visitors: contact in advance.

Craigmillar Park
1 Observatory Rd.
Tel: 0131 667 0047
Parkland course, with good views. 18 holes, 5,851yds, Par 70.
Visitors: must contact in advance, may not play weekends and after 3.30pm weekdays.

Dalmahoy Hotel Golf & Country Club
Kirknewton. Tel: 0131 333 1845

Two upland courses, one Championship. East course: 18 holes, 6,677yds, Par 72. West course: 18 holes, 5,185yds, Par 68.
Visitors: weekend by application.

Duddingston
Duddingston Rd West.
Tel: 0131 661 7688
Parkland, semi-seaside course with burn as a natural hazard. Easy walking and windy. 18 holes, 6,647yds, Par 72.
Visitors: may not play at weekends.

Kingsknowe
326 Lanark Rd. Tel: 0131 441 1145
Hilly parkland course with prevailing SW winds. 18 holes, 5,979yds, Par 69.
Visitors: contact in advance and subject to availability of tee times.

Liberton
297 Gilmerton Rd.
Tel: 0131 664 3009
Undulating, wooded parkland course. 18 holes, 5,299yds, Par 67.
Visitors: may only play before 5pm on Tue & Thu Apr-Sep. Must contact in advance.

Lothianburn
106A Biggar Rd, Fairmilehead. Tel: 0131 445 2206 & 0131 445 5067
Hillside course with a 'T' shaped wooded-area, situated in the Pentland foothills. Sheep on course. Testing in

windy conditions. 18 holes,
5,750yds, Par 71.
Visitors: weekends after 3.30pm
contact professional, weekdays up
to 4pm.

Merchants of Edinburgh
10 Craighill Gardens.
Tel: 0131 447 1219
Testing hill course. 18 holes,
4,889mtrs, Par 65.
Visitors: must play with member at
weekends.

Mortonhall
231 Braid Rd. Tel: 0131 447 6974
Moorland course with views over
Edinburgh. 18 holes, 6,557yds,
Par 72.
Visitors: advisable to contact by
phone.

Murrayfield
43 Murrayfield Rd.
Tel: 0131 337 3478
Parkland course on the side of
Corstophine Hill, with fine views. 18
holes, 5,725yds, Par 70.
Visitors: contact in advance, may not
play at weekends.

Portobello
Stanley St. Tel: 0131 669 4361
Public parkland course, easy walking.
9 holes, 2,400yds, Par 32.
Visitors: may not play Sat 8.30-10am &
12.30-2pm and on competition days.

Prestonfield
Prestonfield Rd North.
Tel: 0131 667 9665
Parkland course with beautiful views.
18 holes, 6,212yds, Par 70.
Visitors: contact secretary in advance.

Ravelston
24 Ravelston Dykes Rd.

Tel: 0131 315 2486
Parkland course. 9 holes, 5,200yds,
Par 66.
Visitors: must contact in advance but
may not play at weekends & bank
holidays.
Royal Burgess
181 Whitehouse Rd, Barnton.
Tel: 0131 339 2075
The Royal Burgess, which was
instituted in 1735, is the oldest golfing
society in the world. Its course is a
pleasant parkland, with much variety.
18 holes, 6,111yds, Par 71.
Visitors: must contact in advance.
Gentlemen only.

Silverknowes
Silverknowes, Parkway.
Tel: 0131 336 3843
Public links course on coast
overlooking the Firth of Forth. 18
holes, 6,216yds, Par 71.
Visitors: restricted Sat & Sun

Swanston
111 Swanston Road, Fairmilehead.
Tel: 0131 445 2239
Hillside course with steep climb at
12th & 13th holes. 18 holes,
5,024yds, Par 66.
Visitors: must contact in advance.

Torphin Hill
Torphin Rd, Colinton.
Tel: 0131 441 1100
Beautiful hillside, heathland course,
with fine views of Edinburgh and the
Forth Estuary 18 holes, 4, 580 mtrs,
Par 67.
Visitors: must contact in advance.

Turnhouse
154 Turnhouse Rd.
Tel: 0131 339 1014
Hilly, parkland/heathland course,
good views. 18 holes, 5,622yds,

Par 69.
Visitors: may not play at weekends
or Wed.

Other courses
Coldstream
Hirsel
Kelso Rd. Tel: 01890 882678
& 883052
Parkland course, with hard walking and
sheltered trees. 18 holes, 6,092yds,
Par 70.
Visitors: contact for details.

Dunbar
Dunbar
East Links. Tel: 01368 862317
Another of Scotland's old links. It is said
that it was some Dunbar members who
first took the game to England. The club
dates back to 1856. The wind, if
blowing from the sea, is a problem. 18
holes, 6,426yds, Par 71.
Visitors: may not play Thu, between
12.30-2 weekdays, 12-2 weekends or
before 9.30am any day.

Duns
Duns
Longformacus Rd. Tel: 01361 882717
& 882194
Interesting upland course, with natural
hazards of water and hilly slopes. Views
south to the Cheviot Hills.
9 holes, 5,864yds, Par 68.
Visitors: welcome except competition
days and Mon, Tue and Wed after 3pm.

Eyemouth
Eyemouth
Gunsgreen House.
Tel: 01890 750551
With the exception of a steep climb on
the 1st tee, this is a compact, flat and
popular seaside course. Fast smooth
greens and fine views are typified by
the 15th, played from an elevated tee to

a green on a peninsula over a North Sea inlet. 9 holes, 4,608mtrs, Par 66. Visitors: may not play before 10.30am Sat or noon Sun.

Galashiels

Galashiels
Ladhope Recreation Ground.
Tel: 01896 753724
Hillside course, superb views from the top; 10th hole very steep. 18 holes, 5,185yds, Par 67.
Visitors: must contact the secretary in advance especially for weekends.

Torwoodlee

Tel: 01896 752260
Parkland course with natural hazards, designed by James Braid. 18 holes, 6,200yds, Par 70.
Visitors: restricted Thu–ladies day and Sat–mens competitions.

Gullane

Gullane. Tel: 01620 842255
Gullane is a delightful village and one of Scotland's great golf centres. Gullane club was formed in 1882. There are three courses and the No 1 is of championship standard. It differs from most Scottish courses in as much as it is of the downland type and hilly. The views from the top of the course are magnificent. Course No 1: 18 holes, 6,466yds, Par 71. Course No 2: 18 holes, 6,244yds, Par 71. Course No 3: 18 holes, 5,251yds, Par 68.
Visitors: advance booking recommended.

Hawick

Hawick
Vertish Hill. Tel: 01450 372293
Hill course with good views. 18 holes, 5,929yds, Par 68.
Visitors: must contact in advance.

Innerleithen

Innerleithen
Leithen Water, Leithen Rd.
Tel: 01896 830951
Moorland course, with easy walking. Burns and rivers are natural hazards. 9 holes, 6,056yds, Par 70.
Visitors: advisable to check for availability for weekends.

Jedburgh

Jedburgh
Dunion Rd. Tel: 01835 863587
Undulating parkland course, windy, with young trees. 9 holes, 5,760yds, Par 68.
Visitors: restricted at weekends during competitions.

Kelso

Kelso
Racecourse Rd. Tel: 01573 223009
Parkland course. Easy walking. 18 holes, 6,046yds, Par 70.
Visitors: advisable to telephone in advance.

Longniddry

Longniddry
Links Rd. Tel: 01875 852141
Undulating seaside links and partial parkland. One of the numerous courses which stretch east from Edinburgh to Dunbar. The inward half is more open and less testing than the wooded outward half. 18 holes, 6,219yds, Par 69.
Visitors: may book tee times up to 7 days in advance, welcome most times except during competitions.

Melrose

Melrose
Dingleton. Tel: 01896 822855 & 822391
Undulating tree-lined fairways with splendid views. 9 holes, 5,579yds,

Par 70.
Visitors: competitions all Sats and many Suns Apr-Oct, ladies priority Tue, junior priority Wed am in holidays.

Minto

Minto
Denholm. Tel: 01450 870220
Pleasant, undulating parkland course featuring mature trees and panoramic views of Scottish Border country. Short but testing. 18 holes, 5,460yds, Par 68.
Visitors: advisable to telephone in advance, and essential for weekends.

Newcastleton

Newcastleton
Holm Hill. Tel: 01387 375257
Hill course. 9 holes, 5,748yds, Par 70.
Visitors: contact in advance.

Peebles

Peebles
Kirkland St. Tel: 01721 720197
Parkland course with fine views. 18 holes, 6,160yds, Par 70.
Visitors: must contact in advance, may not play Sat.

Selkirk

Selkirk
Selkirk Hill. Tel: 01750 22508
Pleasant moorland course set around Selkirk Hill. Unrivalled views. 9 holes, 5,620yds, Par 68.
Visitors: may not play Mon evening, competition/match days.

ACTIVITIES

TOURIST INFORMATION CENTRES

Coldstream *
The Town Hall
76 High Street
Tel: 01890 882607

Dalkeith*
Dalkeith Library
White Hart Street
Tel: 0131 663 2083

Dunbar
143 High Street
Tel: 01368 863353

Edinburgh
Edinburgh and Lothians
4 Rothesay Terrace
Tel: 0131 226 6800

Edinburgh and Scotland
3 Princes Street
Tel: 0131 557 1700

Edinburgh Airport
Ingliston
Tel: 0131 333 2167
Haddington

31 Court Street
Tel: 01602 827422

Hawick*
Drumlanrig's Tower
Tel: 01450 372547

Jedburgh
Murrays Green
Tel: 01835 863435

Kelso*
The Town Hall
The Square
Tel: 01573 223464

Linlithgow
Burgh Halls
The Cross
Tel: 01506 844600

Melrose*
Abbey House
Abbey Street
Tel: 01896 822555

Newtongrange*
Scottish Mining Museum

Lady Victoria Colliery
Tel: 0131 663 4262

North Berwick
1 Quality Street
Tel: 01602 892197

Oldcraighall
by Musselburgh
Tel: 0131 653 6172

Peebles
23 High Street
Tel: 01721 720138

Penicuik*
Edinburgh Crystal Visitor Centre
Eastfield
Tel: 01968 673846

Selkirk*
Halliwells House
Tel: 01750 20054

*Denotes seasonal opening only

INDEX

ACKNOWLEDGEMENTS

The Automobile Association wishes to thank the following photographers and libraries for their assistance in the preparation of this book.

J M BAXTER 46, 84
NATURE PHOTOGRAPHERS LTD, E A Janes 75

The remaining photographs are held in the Association's own library, (AA PHOTO LIBRARY) and were taken by
M Alexander 10/11, 41, 46/7, 52, 54, 58/9, 89; J Beazley 14/5, 38, 65, 66, 85, 86; P&G Bowater 28;
D Corrance 17, 23, 26/7, 42, 58, 62/3, 77, 81, 83; C Lees 8, 90; S&O Matthews 36/7, 58/9; K Patterson 7, 13,
18/9, 20/1, 32, 33, 34, 35, 39, 40, 41, 49, 50, 56, 69, 72, 88a, 88b; M Taylor 22, 71

Cover photographs

ANDY WILLIAMS PHOTO LIBRARY front – main
INTERNATIONAL PHOTOBANK back – top
D Corrance: back – middle
J A Tims: front (walkers)